Radical Community Work

Perspectives from Practice in Scotland

Edited by
Ian Cooke and Mae Shaw

for Kieran, Kirsty and Ruari

Published by Moray House Institute of Education,
Holyrood Road, Edinburgh EH8 8AQ

First published 1996
First Reprint 1997

ISBN 0 901580 81 3
© 1996 Ian Cooke and Mae Shaw

Printed and bound in Great Britain by
Redwood Books, Trowbridge, Wiltshire

Contents

Foreword

THIS BOOK is particularly timely, as community work is being 'rediscovered', and taken up, in the words of Professor Gary Craig, Editor of the Community Development Journal, as a 'potential panacea for political and economic dislocation'. In the current context, community development approaches are being promoted for a wide variety of reasons. Policy-makers, with widely differing perspectives, seem to be agreed on the relevance of community-based strategies. There has been a plethora of community-based approaches to improve service delivery, and to promote self-help and voluntary effort, in the mixed economy of welfare. There has also been increasing focus upon community-based strategies to combat poverty and to promote 'community participation' and 'empowerment'. This 'fashionable rhetoric' of 'community', as it has been described by Professor Alan Barr, including the recent focus upon the new 'communitarianism', has been a major feature of debates on both sides of the Atlantic. This has also been an increasing feature in debates about participation and development in the Third World.

'Radical Community Work: Perspectives from Practice in Scotland' grapples with these underlying debates. The book starts from the vital importance of providing a critical framework for analysis. Key concepts are examined, so that the reader can unravel the ways in which terminology is being hi-jacked. This sets the framework for the development of a new paradigm, starting from the potential opportunities of the contemporary economic, political, social and cultural climate, whilst providing a critical analysis of its constraints.

This book is so particularly valuable, though, because these theoretical debates are so firmly rooted in the critical analysis of contemporary practice. Separate chapters focus upon learning from practice reflectively, within a number of settings. There is a focus on learning from community work strategies for combating disadvantage and exclusion, and for analysing the limitations of experiences of partnerships for tackling issues of poverty and promoting urban regeneration. Examples of practice issues range over a broad spectrum. They include the lessons of anti-poll tax campaigning for direct action, political education and the development of alliances for social justice. And they include the possibilities of developing radical community work practice in fields which have often been defined as falling within the remit of social work, rather than community work; fields such as community care and work with lone parents. Throughout there is an active critical engagement too, with the importance of Solidarity in Difference, developing an understanding of class which is not reductionist and developing an understanding of oppression at both local and global levels.

The depth as well as the breadth of these experiences relates to the specific context for this collection, rooted as it is in Scottish community work. This reflects both the extent of Scottish experiences, and the level of critical reflection in Scotland, a factor which has been both reflected in and stimulated by initiatives such as the journal *Concept*. Over the five year period of its life, *Concept* has become the major Scottish community education publication, linking community education with community work more generally. This richness of the Scottish scene makes this book so useful to practitioners and students, more widely.

In addition, this book will be vital reading for a wide variety of policy makers and professionals who, increasingly, need to relate their work to local communities. As Professor David Donnison has pointed out, so aptly, community-based ways of working have exerted vital influences on other professions and services and this, in turn, raises key questions about how to build critical reflections on these developments into their professional education and training. Whilst there have been a number of important publications in this field, over the last year or so, there is still a shortage of critical materials, and especially of critical materials linking theoretical debates with practice experiences. This book represents a major step towards remedying this gap, both for community workers, and other professionals and policy-makers, and for the wider audience of those who are active in their own communities.

Marjorie Mayo
Senior Lecturer
Goldsmith's College, London

Introduction

Community work can be seen to be the product of two sets of forces and interests which reflect the changing context of political relations in society. The first is pressure from below, which stems broadly from democratic aspiration, the other from above, reflecting the changing needs of the state and broader political interests. This dialectical relationship has, traditionally, been the focus for the practice of radical community work, which has concentrated on exposing the contradictions and working creatively within them (see, for example, Baldock, 1977; Craig, 1989).

This collection demonstrates a continuity in this dialectical thinking, recognising that the nature of the contradictions are contingent on context. In this sense, the collection raises issues and possibilities which are particular to the circumstances of the 1990s and the policy and political context which has given rise to them.

Whilst the context is a new one, many of the chapters are essentially historical – locating issues within the development of social and economic relations which constitute advanced welfare capitalism. The global restructuring of capital is, in this way, connected with the experience of communities affected by the processes of marketisation, deregulation and commodification, whether in relation to housing (Doyle et al), economic regeneration (Player, Collins and Lister) or welfare (Shaw). There is also a recognition that the oppositional paradigms of community work which have emerged historically need to be reformulated in order to reconnect the politics of position with the politics of identity (Cooke, Meagher and Tett). The role of the community worker as a professional, in the best sense of the term, is broadly defined as critical, competent and creative (Rosendale).

Most of the contributions reflect an impatience to move beyond critique, which has characterised community work over the past decade, towards the construction of an alternative agenda, and the 'language of possibility'. In this sense, they are essentially practical (as distinct from pragmatic), grounded in theoretical and political understanding. Many reflect the necessity to engage with a more complex policy context and the need to be vigilant about the way in which interests can be obscured by the language of 'community'. A recurring theme is the use, misuse or appropriation of language. Language as a site of contest and struggle raises issues about the possibility or desirability of reclaiming it, exploiting its ambiguity, forcing it to live up to its promise, exposing the shallowness of its application, or rejecting it for an alternative discourse which allows for the possibility of human agency (Collins and Lister, Rosendale, Player, Doyle et al, Shaw, Petrie, Orton).

The narrowing of the discourse of 'freedom' and 'responsibility', a key feature of the hegemonic project of the new right which has dominated the political terrain since 1979, is highlighted in the way in which communities have been presented with a singular view of the world; in which individualised problems require individualised solutions; where non-conformity to the hegemonic ideal carries the stigmata of failure, either requiring punitive action (Findlay) or is internalised to the disadvantage of those concerned (Meagher and Tett, Petrie). It is argued that hegemony by consent has been replaced by a 'hegemony of resignation' (Milliband, 1994) in which power is exercised by the limiting of perceptions of possibility – the view that there is no alternative. The need to challenge 'common sense' assumptions and offer alternative problem definitions is therefore addressed in all the chapters.

Central to the task of assisting groups to define issues and problems for themselves is the crucial notion of 'voice'. This extends definitions and explanations to the recognition and reclaiming of subjugated cultures and histories, and should be a characteristic of all progressive community work practice (Orton, Meagher and Tett, Arshad).

The advent of 'identity politics' is addressed in several chapters, some presenting the unarguable case for sensitivity to the differential experiences of particular marginalised groups, others arguing that the constituency of 'community' should be redefined to avoid closure and exclusion – that the health of communities (plural) is a pre-requisite for the health of the community as a whole (Doyle et al, Arshad, Petrie, Shaw).

Community conceived solely as neighbourhood is challenged implicitly in a number of the chapters (Petrie, Meagher and Tett, Arshad), though some contributors argue that locality is still a legitimate and highly effective focus for connecting issues of identity with those of material position (Cooke). Locality need not necessarily equate with competitive localism (Player) but, as the site in which the contradictions of policy are exposed, it offers opportunities for connecting the local with the broader context, (Doyle et al) and the personal with the political (Findlay).

The difficulties of reconciling difference with solidarity exercises many of the authors, who see the necessity of acknowledging and engaging with difference whilst forging a unity on the basis of which to address overarching material inequalities. (Shaw, Cooke). There is a broad recognition of multiple identities which must articulate with each other, but a case is made for solidarity in difference, which recognises the need to ground issues of identity in material experience and position. The mediation of class by other identities and vice versa is explored in a number of chapters. There is therefore a concern to reject reductionist or one-dimensional accounts of human experience, whilst recognising the need to acknowledge the primacy of economic relationships in determining the conditions of people's lives.

The emergence of a popular politics which seems to eschew traditional political forms gives cause for both optimism and concern. Consequently, the book as a whole represents an attempt to engage, on the one hand, with those movements which see cultural politics as having more potential for challenging problem definitions which disadvantage them. On the other hand, it is also necessary to reconnect with and, as necessary, revise those collective political forms which have traditionally engaged directly in the economic sphere. Alliances will therefore be essential if social movements are to be effective in challenging the current social order.

Disillusionment with traditional forces of social change is shared by a number of contributors. In particular, it is acknowledged that the 'new' Labour Party can no longer be assumed to be an ally of marginalised and excluded groups. Nevertheless, the prospect of a change of government in the UK context and the implications of this for the political scene in Scotland, offer the possibility of creating a politics to foster a collectivism which expresses the socialist principles of egalitarianism and democracy (Cooke, Doyle et al).

The absence of a coherent political project, it is claimed, inhibits the development of a more radical paradigm in community work. However, whilst it is still the case that the community work contribution will not be the decisive one, the current context, with its fluid political forms and the centrality of community to both the policy context and the formation of social movements, puts community workers in a potentially key position to foster and support those ideas and organisations which may form the basis of a more unified, progressive politics.

This is a book written from practice – a collection of articles by current community work practitioners or those who, until recently, were directly engaged in the field. For many of us it represents not only a struggle to theorise practice but also to reinstate what we see as a crucial continuity in community work literature: the struggle to create radical paradigms which challenge the technicist agenda of much mainstream policy and practice. Similarly, our wish to assert that it is not our role to deliver 'the community' at every turn of policy seeks to make a distinction between the functions of policy and the purposes of radical community work – to work with autonomous organisations which challenge structural inequalities in a way which politicises everyday experience.

Ian Cooke
Mae Shaw

References

Baldock, P. (1977). Why community action? The historical origins of the radical trend in British community work. *Community Development Journal.* 12(2). Oxford University Press

Craig, G. (1989), Community work and the state. *Community Development Journal.* 24(1). Oxford University Press

Milliband, R. (1994). *Socialism for a Sceptical Age.* Polity Press

Chapter 1: Whatever Happened to the Class of '68? – The Changing Context of Radical Community Work Practice

Ian Cooke

Synopsis

In reasserting the primacy of 'class' as a way of locating explanations of social inequalities, this chapter reviews the claims of and insights gained from the radical analysis which emerged from the Community Development Projects. The author argues, however, that whilst the explanatory force of this analysis remains, the terrain of struggle and range of combatants reflect a dynamic and complex political and social context.

A radical community work practice which seeks to identify transformative opportunities needs to engage with this changing context, connecting the specific experience of new social movements with the common interests addressed by class-based political forms. By reconnecting with historical understandings whilst recognising the development of new social forces, the author argues that common material experience of inequality can act as a catalyst for forging unity out of difference. The issue of poverty, it is argued, presents a major opportunity for the development of a political analysis which connects with people's common lived experience. Arguing for systematic reflection and purposeful educational processes, the article identifies a radical community work practice which is critical, competent and creative.

Introduction

Despite the rhetoric surrounding it, community work is not an inherently radical activity. In fact several studies, including in a Scottish context those of Alan Barr (1987 & 1991), have demonstrated that community work is more often about continuity than change. Nonetheless, there has been an important, if minority, tradition within community work since the early seventies which takes cognizance of the wider societal context and attempts to develop a relevant and progressive practice. This chapter seeks to explore both radical community work and the context in which it occurs, with a view to contributing to a debate about possibilities and problems rather than providing definitive answers. In doing so it does not claim to offer original thinking but, rather, draws unashamedly on a variety of sources ranging from community work colleagues to some 'classic' community work texts, all of which have influenced both my thinking and practice.

The world as it is

Writing in 1962, Alinsky claimed that the basic requirement for the politics of change was to 'recognise the world as it is. We must work with it on its own terms if we are to change it to the kind of world we would like to see'. In a UK context the only real challenge to the dominant social welfare paradigm of community work emerged from the Community Development Projects (CDPs), set up in 1968 and developed throughout the following decade. It was a notion which, whilst recognising the historical role of community work as a controlling force within society, believed that it was possible to develop both an analysis and practice which would allow community workers to serve, rather than work against, the interests of the local communities within which they were located. Community work practised in this way sought to make a contribution, albeit a marginal one, to some kind of progressive social change based on a view of how that change would come about. It therefore seems essential that any re-evaluation of the concept of 'radical' community work must, by definition, involve a re-evaluation of the ever changing social, economic and political context in which community work has been, and continues to be practised.

It is the contention of this chapter that clarity about the contribution of community work to the broader political project was key to the development of a practice which located community work within theories of the state, and that it is the current lack of clarity and direction which hinders the further development of a coherent radical practice for the 1990s and beyond. As Meekosha (1993) points out ' ... for many practitioners and community activists there is no longer one story to guide them. There is no agreement on the ends or the processes, or indeed who constitutes the enemy'. Unless some clarity and consensus on the broader political project is re-established

,ose community workers who seek to consciously develop a / practice will work in an increasingly fragmented way, ano... ng even further the marginal contribution which community work can make towards some form of progressive social change.

When we look at the wider context in which community work operates we see not only dramatic changes since those heady days when a radical critique was first developed, but we also witness a pace of change which has left most practitioners reeling. The change has had two distinct, but connected, features. Firstly, a major restructuring of international capital, with a Conservative Government in the UK which has abandoned post-war consensus around the Welfare State and embarked on a political project to 'roll back the state', replacing it with internal and external markets. Secondly, we have witnessed the undermining and dilution of what was once seen by many as the major force for radical economic, political and social change – the Labour and Trade Union movement. We have also seen the emergence and development of 'new social movements' over a twenty year period and, latterly, increasing evidence of a more spontaneous and fragmented direct action type of pressure group politics, much of which focuses around environmental issues. Community workers need to analyse both this changing context and the processes of tranformative change if a refined practice based on the contribution which community work can make to those processes is to be developed.

Developing a radical analysis and practice

The analysis which emerged from the CDPs, acknowledging the dubious historical function of community development, and locating community work within theories of the state, is well documented elsewhere (see Mayo, 1975, Craig, 1989). For the purposes of this chapter, however, it is important to highlight one or two aspects which particularly influenced the development of practice.

Many of the workers within the CDPs increasingly came to recognise that the causes of the 'social problems' which they were established in communities to tackle, did not in fact originate within, nor were they distinct to, those communities. These areas, they argued, 'typified structural processes taking place in working class communities throughout Britain' (Green, 1992). This analysis challenged the established orthodoxy which defined community work as: 'a process by which a community identifies its needs ..., orders these needs ..., finds the resources ..., to deal with these needs

..., takes action in respect of them and, in so doing, extends and develops co-operative and collaborative attitudes and practices in the community' (Ross, in Craig, 1989).

It also had important implications for community work practice. Firstly, it was argued, the boundaries drawn around these communities were not only, in many cases, artificial but were drawn in fact to internalise the issues and problems so that solutions were sought from within those hard pressed communities, obscuring the structural nature of the problems. It was therefore essential that radical community work sought to 'break down' those boundaries. Secondly, if the causes of those problems were structural in nature then clearly they could not simply be resolved by the introduction of community workers. Given the political and economic context of the time, the message was clear: a radical practice, if it was to affect any change at all 'must align itself with class politics aimed at restructuring the economic, political and social system' (Thorpe, 1985). The aim of community work which emerged from this analysis was to encourage community groups to go beyond their locality, to link with other groups, and the organised labour movement and to engage in collective action.

Whilst many community workers organised local people around issues and supported a range of campaigning activities, what differentiated radical from pluralist practice was this core aim of encouraging community groups to link beyond their immediate geographical boundaries and with the broader Trade Union and Labour movement. By being involved in this way around issues of concern, it was argued, local people and community groups would be more likely to understand the real origin and nature of the issues and problems they faced, possible solutions to these problems and, ultimately, options for affecting wider social change – in short, a political analysis. In recognising the limitations of community work intervention, this position rejected the notion of a community work practice whose aim was the resolution of problems and issues and saw instead its major aim (in a Marxian sense) as political consciousness raising by highlighting rather than resolving the contradictions.

The broader radical project of the time was the development of the rank and file shop stewards' movement within the Trade Unions and the advance of 'the left' within the Labour Party, promoting and winning support for socialist policies. The combined Labour and Trade Union movement were, in this account, regarded as the prime force of social, political and economic change. There was, therefore, no real need to establish and develop a 'community wing' within the broader Labour movement or any kind of sustainable community movement. The aim was the development of 'politicised' activists who, it was argued, would make a greater and more effective contribution from within the Labour and Trade Union movement: 'What consciousness can be aroused in such struggles will remain sectional unless it is keyed into an embracing political strategy involving all the poor, all the ill housed, all the deprived.' (Coates, quoted in Mayo, 1975)

Reflections: strengths and weaknesses

That a number of community workers and community work projects encouraged and supported the development of collective action beyond immediate geographical boundaries is undeniable. From the 1970s onwards community groups, supported by community workers, formed alliances over a range of issues, with perhaps the most concentrated and consistent involvement in the Scottish context being around the issue of housing. While some of this work is discussed elsewhere in this book (see Doyle et al) it does seem important, for the purposes of this chapter, to acknowledge the number of tenant alliances, federations and city-wide action groups which have taken up a wide range of housing issues throughout Scotland over the last 25 years. There are, for example, currently twenty tenants' federations active in Scotland and community workers have contributed greatly to that level of activity. As recently as 1988 over 3,000 tenants from throughout the central belt of Scotland marched along Edinburgh's Princes Street in opposition to the 'Scottish Homes' legislation – a turnout that was in part due to the networking of like-minded community workers.

However, the extent of links between community groups and the Labour and Trade Union movement, so central to the CDP analysis, is far less convincing. There is no doubt that some links were achieved and some alliances formed but these links between community groups and the labour movement were far less frequent and the quality far more tenuous than those between community groups themselves. There are, I believe, a number of reasons for this major weakness in applying the analysis to practice. At a practical level, developing credibility and making links with the Trade Union movement was often a long-term project which did not lend itself to the inherent 'short termism' of much community work and, whilst community work projects with a shared radical approach and sufficient staff could allocate some time to this task, (mainly using their trade union credentials to become delegates to Trades Councils as a way of developing credibility and contacts) this was much more difficult for workers who were geographically isolated or isolated politically within their workplace. In addition, despite efforts on the part of some community workers to seek out sympathetic contacts, initial attempts to link community groups with the Labour movement were often characterised by a lukewarm response from Trade Union representatives. This was perhaps not surprising, in that many of these Labour and Trade Union representatives shared a not dissimilar analysis to that which emerged from the CDPs in that they also recognised the relatively greater bargaining power of organised labour and thus accorded links with community groups much less 'priority' than other activities in which they were involved. Finally, the 'roller coaster' short-term nature of community activity was often incompatible with the formalised processes of the Labour and Trade Union movement.

The significance of these difficulties in linkage was that they made the aim of developing class-consciousness problematic; particularly when, throughout the period in question, many of the community campaigns were directed against Labour governments and Labour-controlled local authorities. Cockburn (1977) highlights an additional problem when 'the class that owns capital, controls land, employs workers, collects rents and interest on the mortgage, the real dominant class, is in the main, invisible within that community'. Although Cockburn was writing in the context of Lambeth, the point has probably even greater significance for the Scottish experience, when one contrasts the Scottish peripheral housing estates with the inner city areas of England.

Alinsky (1962) points out that 'happenings become experiences when they are digested, when they are reflected upon, related to general patterns and synthesised'. If reflection was the key to analysing some of the contradictions and difficulties, there is little evidence to suggest that community work practice, certainly in the Scottish context, managed to incorporate thorough and systematic reflection. In fact the engagement of activists and community groups in reflection largely took place in an opportunistic and piecemeal way. This weakness I believe stemmed from a lack of attention paid to theoretical understandings of educational development and, compounding this, a community work approach in which the educational role of the worker was revealed gradually, in many instances only becoming explicit well into the process. The latter factor was often the result of a pragmatic decision which recognised that successful community work intervention depended on achieving 'credibility' within a relatively short space of time.

The changing context of practice

It is difficult to summarise the major social and political developments of the last two decades but it could be argued that two developments in particular had a major impact on the focus of radical community work practice. Firstly, 1974 witnessed the first cuts in public sector funding by the then Labour Government, leading to over 20 years of further reduction in public spending by successive governments. This period proved to be a key influence on the development of community work for two reasons. Prior to 1974, as Waddington (1979) points out 'successful localised campaigns fed off the annual surplus of a growing economy and were part of a system of public sector redistribution to disadvantaged and marginal groups. This provided the baits which were the initial stimulus for community action'. In addition, this attack on the welfare state led to a re-focusing of community work in that services, which had rightly been 'attacked' prior to 1974 for the way in which they were delivered, now increasingly had to be defended. Secondly, these problems were further compounded with the election of the first Thatcher Government in 1979, causing the struggle to widen from a resource battle to an ideological one. Four terms of Conservative rule have also seen a profound centralisation of power and resources, again creating further difficulties for community work operating at a local level.

Whilst these factors all contributed to confusion for the development of a radical community work practice, the major contextual change was the question of what now constituted the broader political project. To address this issue we need to examine what has happened to the traditional forces of social change which were so crucial to the radical analysis of the CDP workers, assess what possibilities new or emerging forces of change offer and, in light of this analysis, determine what offers the best prospects for social transformation.

It was, ironically, the unambiguous class analysis of the New Right which ensured that, when the Conservatives came to power in 1979, the emasculation of the Labour and Trade Union movement would be a central objective, reflecting a view that 'without labour movements organised as political forces, no fundamental challenge to the existing social order can ever be mounted' (Milliband, 1989). In retrospect, there seems to have been three main aspects of this policy, the first and most far-reaching being a succession of anti-Trade Union legislation. The effectiveness of these measures was greatly assisted by the creation of mass unemployment which rose quickly from 1 to 3.5 million and this was compounded by the ideological promotion of self -interest, individualism and competition. These measures allowed the Government to take on and defeat one group of the most organised workers after another, the watershed being the defeat of the National Union of Mineworkers (NUM) in 1985. In addition, the restructuring of capital which has swept throughout Europe, has decimated the industries and areas of employment which were once the power base of the Trade Union movement, presenting serious challenges to the effectiveness and strength of any future trade union movement.

Any re-emergence of a strong trade union movement would seem, critically, to depend on its ability to organise in the less traditional areas of local government and the health service, the banking and insurance industry and the mushrooming service sector which has long been notoriously difficult to organise. With patterns of employment, nationally, moving towards more part-time, temporary and casualised employment, the challenges facing the trade union movement are not inconsiderable. Historically, the basis of a strong Trade Union movement has been the level of local organisation and any recovery may well depend upon the resurgence of the kind of rank and file shop steward activity which has characterised the most effective periods of trade union organisation. Given that it has only been at times of high levels of organisation and confidence – often coinciding with low levels of unemployment – that the trade unions have been able to move beyond narrow sectional economic interests, their role or potential role as a force of social change rests heavily on their ability to meet the kind of challenges highlighted above.

It is the view of this author that the role of the Labour Party leadership throughout this changing context has been both misguided and dishonourable, often preferring to undermine rather than support the kinds of struggles which created the Labour Party in the first place. The 'modernisation' of the Labour Party since the mid- 1980s has seen the ditching of one socialist policy after another, the abandonment of Clause Four and the general distancing of itself from the Trade Unions (if not their financial support). Lashar (1994) claims 'the middle class has seized hold of the Labour Party and is preventing it carrying out its original task – the redistribution of wealth'. This rightward shift of the Labour Party has progressed to such an extent that Labour can no longer automatically assume the 'radical' mantle amongst British political parties and, in the narrower Scottish context, this situation is even more pronounced with the Scottish National Party clearly having a more overtly socialist programme than Labour (unilateral nuclear disarmament, re-nationalisation of public utilities, restoration of benefits to 16/17 year olds, restoration of student grants, and so on). Whilst it seems likely that the Labour Party could well form the next UK Government, they must clearly be regarded as a force to maintain the status quo rather than a force for progressive change.

At a local political level, the optimism and ambition of a number of Labour-controlled councils in the late 1970s/early 1980s who shunned the 'dented shield' strategy (better Labour cuts than Tory cuts!) of the national Labour Party leadership and sought to develop local government as a base for the implementation of socialist policies and, in some cases as an arena for class struggle, has given way to a pragmatic approach where the major ambition is to minimise the scale and impact of spending cuts. Whilst it would have to be acknowledged that, in a Scottish context, a combination of labour-dominated local authorities and the lack of Scottish Conservative M.P.s seems to have resulted in Scottish councils faring better, relatively speaking, than their English counterparts, the ease with which the Scottish Office was able to totally re-organise local government without any effective resistance, gives some indication of the current strength and direction of municipal socialism (or, as it is now, municipal capitalism!).

New social movements

Whilst the traditional forces of social change have clearly declined, however, other groupings have emerged during a not dissimilar period and, in the context of this article, certainly need to be considered. Since the emergence of the Women's Movement in the

1960s, we have seen a range of movements built around the concerns of black people, gays and lesbians, and the disabled – linking the personal with the political. These 'new social movements' have had a marked impact throughout society and it is to their potential as a force, or forces, for transformative social change that we must turn, including their relationship with the traditional forces of social change. Oliver (1990) writes: 'it has to be admitted that nowhere in the world have these new movements been successful in overturning the status quo. Their significance has been in placing new issues on the political agenda, in presenting old issues in new forms and indeed in opening up new arenas of political discourse'. The fundamental problem, as Oliver sees it is that the, in some cases, significant gains made by these new social movements have occurred within civil society and, thus, in order for them to become a significant force of societal change, one of two things must happen. There has to be either a transfer of power from the state political institutions to civil society which, despite cosmetic attempts such as the Citizen's Charter, looks unlikely in the foreseeable future; or social movements have to exert greater influence over state political institutions.

A number of commentators (see Arshad in this volume) have highlighted the fractionalised nature of identity politics and more recently criticism has focussed around the implications of overlapping identities and the challenges they, in turn, present to the respective social movements. But, in the context of this chapter, an increasingly important criticism is that made by Croft and Beresford (1992) – that the social movements have 'resulted in an over-rapid retreat from class analysis and politics and the possibilities these offer for united action'. This criticism is characterised in the tragic example given by Harvey (1993) of the fire at the Imperial Fords Chicken Processing Plant in Carolina, in which 25 workers died and a further 56 were seriously injured. The broader context in which the tragedy occurred was of increasing control of the Republican Party by big business throughout the 1970s and 1980s, the weakening of working class politics caused partly, claims Harvey, by the 'increasing fragmentation of progressive politics around special issues and the new social movements', and the resultant de-regulation of industry. Despite the fact that most of the workers were women and black, neither the organised feminist nor black movements saw fit to engage politically with what happened and , 'by pursuing mutually exclusive discourses effectively undermined the kind of working class politics which might have protected the interests of gender and race, even if that working class politics regrettably makes no explicit acknowledgement of race and gender'.

In her study of the American feminist movement, Segal (1991) observes that, despite its size and influence, US women have seen the least overall change in the relative disadvantages of their sex, compared to other Western democracies. The huge gains made by the middle and upper classes have been more than offset by the worsening position of working class women in the United States. Therefore, if social movements are to avoid being both merely reformist and elitist they must, as Sivanandan (1989) argues 'derive their politics from the needs, freedoms, rights of the most disadvantaged amongst them'. Social movements can only become forces for transformative social change when they move beyond operating solely within their specific oppression and recognise both the interrelatedness of various oppressions and the need to build effective alliances based upon them (see Arshad, Shaw, Petrie, and Tett and Meagher in this volume). It is here that we return to the issue of class which has the potential to provide the basis for these alliances. 'Class', as Sivanandan states, 'cannot just be a matter of identity, it has to be the focus of commitment'.

Contrary to the assumed irrelevance of 'class' within current political discussion, Lashmar (1994), in comparing a Gallup opinion poll taken in 1945 with a Mori Poll carried out in 1989, points out that far more people regarded themselves as working class than they had done forty years earlier (43% in 1949 : 67% in 1989). This raises the question of why, in the face of the emasculation of the Labour and Trade Union movement and the abandonment of class politics by the national Labour Party leadership, this shift has occurred. The answer, I would argue, can be found in the changes which have taken place within the economy, particularly over the last fifteen years – high levels of unemployment and less job security, growing inequality of both income and wealth and constant attacks on those aspects of the welfare state which were redistributive and universalist in nature. In addition, there is a growing recognition that, despite official attempts to either define poverty out of existence or explain it away in terms of an 'underclass', the scope and levels of poverty, already dramatically high, are set to expand rapidly (see Bennington (1992) and Townsend (1992). This has moved commentators to claim that these increases will force the issue of poverty to the centre of the political agenda in the coming decade. Mainstream newspapers such as the 'Scotsman' have featured articles commenting on the implications of recent European Commission and Bank of England reports. A recent piece by McLaughlin (1995) concluded that 'if all these predictions are correct Europe is heading for a social and political crisis not seen since the last war or the depression before that'.

Solidarity in difference – forging unity

When we consider the fact that women, black people and disabled people figure disproportionately in any poverty statistics (60% of all disabled people for example live in or on the margins of poverty and 75% are reliant on state benefits: source Craig 1990) it seems essential that any re-alignment of social forces of change is based on the centrality of class. Feminist critiques of the radical CDP model of community work stressed the over-emphasis on the mode of production at the expense of the means of reproduction now need to be re-evaluated to take account of the restructuring of the economy and the shifting balance within the forces of change. Twenty years on there is a far greater number of women in paid employment (the majority in low paid jobs and poorly organised workplaces), a greatly weakened position of trade unions, and real possibilities for a more prominent role for 'community' and 'neighbourhood' which recognises the validity of struggle beyond the economic sphere. Sivanandan (1989) points out that the transformation which has taken place within the economy means that capital no longer needs labour as before, explaining why labour has lost much of its economic and, therefore, political clout. The struggle, he argues, must therefore reflect this change by shifting from the economic to the political sphere. Whilst the battle is still over the ownership and control of the means of production and the exploitation of the working class, this exploitation and the resulting inequalities need to be addressed at a political/ ideological level. Contrasting examples of this can be seen in the importance which trade unions now attach to public support for their campaigns and the success of the anti-poll tax campaign fought largely outwith the labour and trade union movement (see Rosendale in this volume).

Whilst there seems little doubt that potential forces of social change are in a fluid situation it is also possible to see the emergence of a new kind of oppositional politics and, more importantly, for the purposes of this chapter how these forces need to change or develop if a transformation of society is to take place. If the social movements recognise the relationship between oppressions and genuinely want to engage in both the economic sphere and the political structures then it seems difficult to imagine how this can be done without the recognition of the centrality of class or 'the 'primacy' of labour movements in regard to social change' as Milliband (1989) refers to it. This position is exemplified by Green politics in that, whilst organisations such as Greenpeace can score significant successes such as the Shell Corporation's U-turn on the disposal of the Brent Spar oil rig, and raise the public profile of other important environmental issues, how do they move to a position where environmental factors begin to suffuse all economic and political decision making? Central to this question is the issue of whether capitalism can be reformed to achieve this, or whether we need to envisage a different form of society where decisions are not taken solely on the basis of profit.

Whilst some of the challenges facing the future of the trade union movement have been noted, in the context of any realignment of the forces of change and the argument for the centrality of class, then it is equally incumbent on the trade union movement to both recognise and respond to the changes which have taken place within society and the new alliances which have to be made. As Blagg and Derricourt (1982) argue '... the labour movement must seek to link its programme with the democratic aspirations of the new movements'. This needs to be done on the basis of the values and traditions which are our inheritance from the working class movement – 'loyalty, comradeship, generosity, or sense of community and a feel for internationalism, an understanding that unity has to be forged and re-forged again and again, and above all, a capacity for making other people's fights one's own.' (Sivanandan 1989).

Whilst the broader political project may be less clear and seem less optimistic than in the 1970s it is the contention of this chapter that the development of a radical practice which takes account of the changing wider context is still possible. It is important to remind ourselves that these changes reflect the constantly evolving nature of society which often occurs at an uneven pace. Similarly, in chronicling the development of socialism, Taylor (1983) reminds us that 'far from following a steady path of theoretical and strategic progress, socialist development has been characterised by fundamental ruptures.' Whilst we seem some way from the merging of the potential forces of change along the lines I have suggested and, importantly, some kind of political manifestation of that fusion, what does seem evident is that this process has to be built from the grass roots.

The anti-poll tax campaign, apart from providing much-needed inspiration, highlighted the democratic deficit which currently haunts Scottish politics. The campaign developed from the growing frustration amongst ordinary people with a situation in which the Scottish electorate consistently and overwhelmingly reject the Conservative Party yet have Conservative policies imposed upon them. This frustration was heightened by what was perceived to be the ineffectiveness and impotence of the Scottish opposition parties, either individually or collectively, to provide some kind of leadership and concerted opposition to Thatcherism in Scotland. After fifteen years the 'wait for the next Labour Government / wait for Independence' response which seems to typifiy mainstream Scottish politics provided the context from which an active rather than a passive type of politics emerged within communities throughout Scotland. The increasing use of direct action tactics by animal rights campaigners, environmentalists and activists from the disabled movement throughout the UK offers further evidence of the fragile emergence of a different kind of politics.

Whilst the support for all kinds of groups taking up and campaigning around issues of concern should be central to any community work practice (see Rosendale in this volume), a radical practice should place emphasis on linking, alliances and solidarity both within and across issues and, at the same time, recognise and act upon the potential for development of a broader political analysis. It is essential that, in shaping a radical practice for the 1990s, we take into account both the strengths and weaknesses of the practice which emerged from the CDPs. For, whilst their structural analysis of economic issues and problems seems as valid today as ever, we need to take into account how capitalism has developed during the intervening period. One outcome of that development, reflected in government, is that the nature of capitalism is now more overt, more visible than it was in the 1970s, when local authorities and welfare state services often seemed to provide a 'buffer' between community campaigns and the interests of capitalism. The operation of the market and the struggle between 'profit' and 'need' is now a key characteristic in many community issues such as housing, health, care and so on (see Doyle et al and Petrie in this volume). However, whilst these developments have clearly had devastating consequences for communities throughout Scotland, ironically they may also offer new opportunities for political consciousness raising (see Shaw in this volume).

Change and uncertainty characterise the context of the early 1990s (see Mayo, 1994) and whilst this fluidity creates difficulties, it also offers both challenges and opportunities – raising the profile and status of community based organisation and campaigns promoting the status of struggle beyond the economic sphere and seeking opportunities for the creative development of new alliances. The radical practitioner in the 1990s must be able to understand the relationship between different oppressions and develop a coherent practice which recognises the contradictory context; identifying and stressing areas of commonality and the opportunistic and creative development of links and alliances between groups.

If the development of a political analysis amongst those with whom we work is still the principal aim of radical community work, it is important to learn from the CDP experience. There is no doubt that people engaged in organising and taking action around issues experience the most dramatic and exciting kind of development (both individual and collective): an awareness of the need to respond to situations collectively, a heightened confidence, an understanding of decision-making, and how to influence it and a range of organisational and campaigning skills. Whilst these are all worthwhile aims, the development of a fuller political analysis can only be achieved by the introduction of systematic reflection and more structured educational opportunities within the community work process; making more explicit to those with whom we work the educational nature of the community work role. Purposeful educational activities such as workshops, conferences and reviewing /planning sessions need to feature more regularly, and be complemented by the creative use of tasks such as making a video or booklet of a campaign to establish adequate reflective space.

When we consider that the success of Thatcherism was founded, in part, on being able to offer the electorate a clear vision in what were (and still are) unsettled times, then community workers should not be afraid of looking at ways in which to introduce alternative views and political ideas to the community work process through these more formal and structured educational activities. The possibility of a fusion between issue-based community work and radical adult education practice is one which has yet to be fully exploited. The development of critical consciousness together with opportunities for activists to synthesise their experiences should be crucial elements in a contemporary radical community work practice.

The CDP analysis stressed the value of developing a historical perspective, not only to contribute to the understanding of issues and problems but also to 'give local people a sense of their own history and their past and potential role as agents of social change' (Green and Chapman, 1992). Whilst links within and between communities of interest are essential to the development of common understanding, the exploration of 'vertical' links with the past enable us to ground political analysis in a way which connects enduring ideas and explanations with contemporary realities. The emphasis on reclaiming subjugated histories within the 'new' social movements demonstrates the importance of this task (see Orton in this volume) and also offers opportunities in enabling people to understand the interrelatedness of oppressions.

Campbell (1993), in rejecting the notion of 'underclass', explains how the term is used to deny any societal or systematic responsibility for poverty and that: 'what it also does is to deny hope and strip impoverished parts of the population of a history, and of a culture. It denies them class belonging, their own class belonging, their own fragmented class connections across a life cycle'. Community workers can challenge this fragmentation and assist these 're-connections' to be made and, therefore, it seems essential that within the development of a contemporary radical practice attention must be paid to the historical context of both issues and organised resistance.

Common experience of poverty: a catalyst for unity

If the convincing arguments of commentators such as Bennington (1992), that increases in levels of poverty will force it to the centre of the political agenda, are to be accepted then the opportunity exists for community work to become far more proactive, organising groups and communities around issues of poverty and the unequal allocation of resources. In this sense the community work task is not 'helping the poor' or trying to 'solve poverty' but instead developing a political analysis of how poverty is created and why it exists. Whilst many community workers claim to be involved in the allocation of resources – from urban aid to the distribution of local authority budgets – the key task here is the addressing of the *political* allocation of resources

– who gets what and on what basis? Whether the community worker is specifically engaged with groups organised around poverty or related issues or with groups organising around issues of identity (womens groups, black groups and so on), an approach focusing on poverty and, importantly, taking action around poverty related issues – would move beyond identity politics to an exploration of a common material experience. For example, a group of disabled people in seeking an explanation of their poverty could identify commonalities as well as the specific experiences arising from disability. Achieving consensus around this kind of community work approach could help redefine a radical practice for the 1990s allowing workers to maximise the marginal contribution of community work by planned and strategic intervention.

If radical community work requires a mission statement for the nineties and beyond then we could do worse than the words of Sivanandan (1989),

> '... to open one's sensibilities out to the oppression of others, the exploitation of others, the injustices and inequalities meted out to others – and to act upon them, making an individual / local case into an issue, turning issues into causes and causes into movements and building in the process a new political culture, new communities of resistance that will take on power and capital and class'.

References

Alinsky, S. D. (1962). *Rules for Radicals*. New York: Vintage Books

Barr, A. (1987). Inside practice – researching community workers in Scotland. *Community Development Journal*. 22(1). Oxford University Press.

Barr, A. (1991). *Practising Community Development*. London: Community Development Foundation

Bennington, J. (1992). Transcript of speech to Concept Seminar 'Community Work and Poverty'. Edinburgh: Moray House

Blagg, H. and Derricourt, N. (1982). Why we need to construct a theory of the state for community work. *In:* Craig et al, eds. *Community Work and the State*. London: Routledge and Kegan Paul

Campbell, B. (1993). Britain's Dangerous Places, transcript of speech to Democratic Left Conference 'New Spirit, New Communities'. Edinburgh

Coates, K.(1975). As quoted in M. Mayo, 'Community development, a radical alternative'. *In:* Bailey and Brake, eds. *Radical Social Work*. Edward Arnold (Publishers) Ltd

Cockburn, C. (1977). *Local Government as Local State*. Pluto Press

Craig, G. (1989). Community Work and the State. *Community Development Journal*. 24(1). Oxford University Press.

Craig, G. (1990). The politics of empowerment in the UK. Paper to Community Development Journal Conference. November

Croft, S. and Beresford, P. (1992). The politics of participation. *Critical Social Policy*. Autumn

Green, J. (1992). The community development project revisited. *In:* Carter, Jeffs and Smith, eds. *Changing Social Work and Welfare*. Buckingham: Open University

Green, J. and Chapman, A. (1992). The British Community Development Projects: lessons for today. *Community Development Journal.* July. Oxford University Press

Harvey, D. (1993). Class relations, social justice and the politics of difference. *In:* J. Squires, ed. *Principal Positions, Post Modernism and the Rediscovery of Value.* London: Lawrence and Wishart

Lashmar, P. (1994). The class of '94. *New Stateman and Society.* October

McLaughlin, C. (1995). Inside Story: Working solutions. *Scotsman.* 15 June

Mayo, M. (1975). Community development, a radical alternative. *In:* Bailey and Brake, ed. *Radical Social Work.* Edward Arnold (Publishers) Ltd

Mayo, M. (1994). *Communities and Caring.* MacMillan

Meekosha, H. (1993). The bodies politic – equality, difference and community practice. *In:* Butcher et al, ed. *Community and Public Policy.* London: Pluto Press in assoc. with CDF and Bradford and Ilkley Community College

Milliband, R. (1989). *Divided Societies.* Oxford University Press

Oliver, M. (1990). *Politics of Disablement.* Basingstoke: MacMillan

Segal, L. (1991). Whose left: socialism, feminism and the future. *New Left Review.* 185

Sivanandan, A. (1990). All that melts into air is solid: the hokum of New Times. *Race and Class.* 31(3)

Taylor, B. (1983). *Eve and the New Jerusalem: Socialism and Feminism in the Nineteenth Century.* London: Virago

Thorpe, R. (1985). Community work and ideology. *In:* Thorpe and Petrucuenia, ed. *Community Work and Social Change.* London: Routledge and Kegan Paul

Townsend, P. (1992). Dangerous Reality of a Two Tier Europe. Transcript of speech delivered at Pilton Partnership Seminar. Edinburgh

Waddington, P. (1979). Looking ahead – community work into the 1980's. *In:* Thomas, ed. *Community Work in the Eighties.* London: National Institute for Social Work, 1983

Chapter 2: Hands Up or Heads Up ? Community Work, Democracy and the Language of 'Partnership'

Chik Collins and Jim Lister

Synopsis

Community work practices prevailing in particular periods can be seen to reflect the wider sociopolitical context in which they are framed. The authors contend that the practice of radical community work in the current context requires an analysis which recognises and engages with the state's dual strategy of increased centralisation of power and control and decentralisation of responsibility. Focusing on 'partnership' areas, they highlight the contradictions between the dominant discourse of 'local democracy' and the experience of it in practice.

It is precisely this disjuncture that presents a fruitful terrain for transformative practice. The rhetorical discourse of 'democracy' offers a way in which language can be constituted as a 'site of struggle and contest'. By reconstituting the meaning of 'partnership' as a critique of its practice, real intentions can be exposed and power relations made explicit.

The chapter highlights the role of community development as potentially either progressive or reactionary – enhancing or diminishing the ability of a community to sustain its own voice in the harsh climate of the 1990s.

Introduction

In the fifteen years between 1964 and 1979 there were a mere four years of Conservative government – from 1970-1974. That Conservative Government was led by Edward Heath on the basis of a nascent monetarist agenda. Faced by working class resistance, most notably in the shipyards of the upper Clyde, Heath succumbed to the infamous 'u-turn' (Foster and Woolfson 1986). Subsequently, Heath's Government was racked by working class militancy on a scale unknown since the 1920s. In 1974 he called an election on the question of who was to run Britain. The electorate's response was to return a Labour Government pledged to 'bring about a fundamental and irreversible shift in the balance of power and wealth in favour of working people and their families' (Labour Party 1973: 7).

The idea of 'radical community work' is one which is strongly rooted in this sociopolitical context (Craig 1989, Ferguson 1992). It was a context which provided political spaces within which that practice could be inserted and developed. However, some twenty years later that context has changed rather dramatically. The Labour Government of 1974 ended in debacle, having utterly failed to deliver on its promises (Coates 1979, 1980). Margaret Thatcher was elected in 1979 and, unlike Heath, she was 'not for turning'. At the time of writing, the Conservatives have continued to rule without interruption. They have sought, with some significant success, to dismantle working class organisations as part of a larger project to remake the sociopolitical context of British capitalism.

Unsurprisingly, this has significantly reduced the political space for the practice of radical community work. As a result, less radical, and ultimately much more 'accommodating' forms of practice have come to the fore. Herein lies the critical irony for all who would seek to promote progressive change in our society. It is much harder to carry out practices which seek to challenge dominant power when that power increases its ascendancy. At the same time, the fact of that increased ascendancy makes the carrying out of those practices all the more vital. The problems posed by such ironies, unfortunately, are not for the faint-hearted.

So, if we are to reassert a radical agenda for community work practice in the rather harsh sociopolitical context of the mid-late 1990s, then we must begin by clarifying the tasks which are involved in that. For us there are two main tasks. The first involves an examination and critique of current and historic models of community work, and their attendant practices. The second involves developing theoretical and practical tools which might strengthen the models and practices of radical community work. However, these tasks are really only separable in analytical terms. For all practical purposes, they are best handled simultaneously. Moreover, if the purposes are to remain practical, then they are best handled from a perspective which is firmly rooted in the actual experience of community development in the current sociopolitical context.

It is from these imperatives that the structure of this paper follows. Within very tight constraints of space, it seeks to handle the tasks of critique and reconstruction simultaneously, and to base both tasks on an engagement with case study material. We should add that this paper is written from a perspective informed by the experience of community development within Strathclyde Region. It is for the reader to decide how far, and in what ways, that experience is relevant to their own area, and their own experience.

Community work and democracy

As we outlined above, the character of community work practices prevailing in particular periods has tended to reflect the wider sociopolitical context within which they are framed. From the end of the 1970s that context was defined by the advent of Thatcherite Conservatism, creating mass unemployment and attacking the power of trades unions and Labour controlled local authorities. In this context Strathclyde developed their Social Strategy for the Eighties (Strathclyde Regional Council 1983). This was essentially an exercise in limiting the damage being inflicted on the most impoverished working class communities – some of which were showing a worrying trend towards social disintegration. And it was one in which community work was allocated a central position. Community work would play a role in helping 'disadvantaged' communities to campaign for a fairer share of the resources which various institutions and agencies, particularly local government, had at their disposal. It would do this by helping to stimulate community leadership (activists) as a focal point for area-based community organisation around these issues of resource distribution. This involved recognizing, at least in theory, the legitimacy of organizing around issues of limited conflict – even when the local authorities themselves were the target (Strathclyde Regional Council 1984).

This approach was, of course, subjected to criticism – not least from community workers who were of a more radical persuasion. Whatever credibility it did have was called into more serious question by the fact that as the years of Conservative rule unfolded and communities became yet more 'disadvantaged', the power and resources of local government, and their ability to do anything to redress disadvantage, were very seriously reduced. Campaigns of the old kind were now much less likely to bear fruit. The desired results were often no longer in the gift of the people whom the traditional strategies for campaigning would target. Increasingly the latter grew impatient with community work practice which seemed to demand of them things which they were not in a position to deliver. The 'enemy', it seemed, had changed. It was more remote, sometimes difficult to identify at all, and certainly more difficult to challenge. How should community work re-orient itself in this newer context ?

It seems that there are two broad agendas. One is to conclude that there is insufficient scope for 'successful' campaigns and that they, and pretty much the whole conflict-oriented approach to community work practice, should be demoted, if not abandoned. In this view, which is that of the Scottish Office, the 'Partnership' areas, and increasingly that of local government itself, community work should become a way of gearing communities into the 'new realities' of the 1990s (e.g. Scottish Office 1988, 1989; Strathclyde Regional Council 1988; Barr 1990; Barr et al 1995. See also Ferguson 1991). What is needed is that they should be brought into 'partnership' with the government (central and local), the voluntary sector and the private sector in order to create areas which can compete for economic prosperity with other locations. Here the term 'partnership' is used – quite deliberately – to mask the unpleasant realities involved in securing the compliance of community organizations with this objective. The goal is not so much community development as 'community *redevelopment*' (a redevelopment which parallels the property redevelopment which usually accompanies it).

The approach we favour is rather different, and rather less prescriptive. It involves trying to address the question of how communities themselves face up to the problem of campaigning to block these moves and to secure a better alternative with more positive outcomes for their own lives, and the role which community workers play in relation to this. Here the answers are less clear, and in many ways more difficult (See Lister/AFTER 1991).

When we approach this question our central concern is democracy – 'real' democracy. This choice is based on considerations of principle, and of strategy. Firstly, as any community worker or community organization worth their salt know, democracy in this sense is not simply about voting. It is about the ability of different groups and classes to exercise collective power in shaping their own futures. Secondly, the question of democracy is the ground on which the various proponents of 'partnership' make their own claims to legitimacy. Partnerships actually claim to be more democratic than the models which they replace. This claim is a strength for so long as it can be sustained. Yet, at the same time, it is a crucial 'Achilles heel'; for it establishes the criteria by which that false claim can be politically exposed and discredited.

But democracy, in our sense, is something which is conspicuous by its absence in the communities we have worked with. So how *can* 'local communities' exert some real and meaningful democratic control over the forces which shape their lives ? Here we believe that the work of Freire remains an important starting point on which to build, and indeed that it is arguably, for the ironic reasons outlined in our introduction, more relevant than ever it was.[1] This belief is not driven by a particular liking for exploring theoretical systems for their own sake, but by our experience and practice. It is to this which we turn first.

Lilybank: campaigning or co-option?

The experience of working with tenants in Lilybank – a small housing scheme (550 houses) in the East End of Glasgow – is an instructive starting point. However, given space constraints, our discussion will have to be brief.[2] Despite being seen as 'a great place to live' by many early tenants, the scheme has borne many of the stigmata characteristic of Glasgow's 'amenity' housing, and has experienced a decline and crisis which is also familiar. Such was the reputation that it came to be seen as 'the scheme that couldn't be community worked'. However, when the scheme was included in one of the East End's Neighbourhood Initiatives in 1991 – and attracted Urban Aid funding – it suddenly became a priority for Social Work management that it *should* be 'community worked'.

The existing Tenants Association in the estate was largely defunct, and was regarded by many tenants with suspicion as to the nature of some of its activities. The only real organised activity amongst the tenants was taking place outside of this structure, and was aimed at saving the local tenants' hall from closure. A campaign was launched, with community work support, and it proved successful. Taking confidence from this, the tenants turned their attention to housing.

1. Compare this point of view on Freire with that of P. V. Taylor in *The Texts of Paulo Freire,* reviewed by Graham Venters in *Concept,* 4.1, 1994: 24-2.

2. An ongoing narrative on developments in the estate is contained in the bi-monthly newsletter of the Cuthelton/Lilybank Tenants' Forum entitled The *Lilybank Lampost.*

They set up a new Tenants' Forum to supplant the defunct and discredited Tenants' Association, and began to campaign quite effectively on housing management issues. The group then began to raise questions of longer term capital investment. Glasgow District Council (GDC) took the position that there would be some money for partial window replacements after about 5 years, but the tenants had something rather more in mind. What the tenants saw as various attempts at placation and obfuscation were made by GDC, but these were seen through and exposed. The campaign continued to gather momentum.

Then GDC's Director of Housing appeared on the scene at a public meeting and pledged a comprehensive redevelopment project for the scheme. The tenants were euphoric. Their campaign, it seemed, had forced a virtual capitulation by the authority. It now appeared that the Forum would have to shift tack from opponents in a straight confrontation to 'partners' in a complex process of 'consultation', for other agencies – Scottish Homes and Parkhead Housing Association – were going to be involved too. This did not seem to pose a particular problem to the tenants at this stage. How, they thought, could these new agencies possibly be worse than GDC?

Yet, with hindsight, the tenants later concluded (in the spring of 1994) that their victory, though based on some great campaigning work, had been more apparent than real. They had, in fact, been outflanked, encircled and co-opted to implementing a pre-negotiated 'carve-up' in which Scottish Homes and Parkhead Housing Association had collaborated with GDC. But hindsight is easy. The important point here is to realise that this was a conclusion which was *reached* by the tenants themselves as a result of their experience. They compared the rhetoric of 'consultation' and 'partnership' with their actual experience of the workings of the process and reached their own conclusions. In this way they began to break through some of the limits which had been imposed on their thought and action when they were earlier outflanked and encircled. Notably, some of the focus of their attention moved from GDC to the Scottish Office and Scottish Homes, and to the relationships between these institutions and central government housing and urban policies.

The problem was that on making this breakthrough much of the most significant damage had already been done. The estate had virtually been cleared, and the redevelopment plans were well advanced. Possibilities for reversing the whole process were quite limited, not least because now GDC and co. were in a position to go in quite hard on the remaining tenants. And so it came to pass that some of the same community members who had been 'partners' participating in the 'consultation process' found themselves, in the Summer of 1995, facing eviction proceedings.

Campaigns: learning and language

Looking at the experience of working in Lilybank we see that the developing campaign is simultaneously an active learning process. As any student of community work knows, this is true of campaigns in general. They always involve more than an attempt to achieve certain specified objectives. Campaigns also involve a process of learning and development within communities whereby the understanding of objectives, their 'deeper' significance, and what is involved in achieving them, can change in significant – and often quite profound – ways.

In Freire's most famous writings (1972a, 1972b) it is these processes of learning and development which take the centre stage. His argument is that a failure to understand the psychology of the learning process which takes place as communities develop generates attempts to lead or impose learning which ultimately do more harm than good. On the other hand, he argues that work which is based on an understanding of this learning process would be an invaluable resource. The idea is that in better understanding the psychology of learning amongst the community, it may be possible to 'catalyse' or 'lubricate' it in some very significant ways.

Freire's view is that in struggling to change their world people also change their understanding of their world. In turn this changes the types of change which they seek and the ways in which they seek it. He sees this as a process in which a group of people *find their own voice* in which they can analyse the world *in their own terms*. It is not surprising, then, that he suggests that if we want to understand the learning process we should pay special attention to the language in which a community speaks, and to the ways in which it changes.[3] This is because language contains and expresses the characteristic and

3. '. . . the object of the investigation is not people (as if people were anatomical fragments), but rather the thought language people use to refer to reality, the level at which they perceive that reality, and their view of the world, which is the source of their generative themes.' (Freire 1972a: 69).
  '. . . the important thing is to detect the starting point at which people visualize the 'given', then verify whether or not during the process of investigation any transformation has occurred in their way of perceiving reality.' (Freire 1972a: 79)

continually developing ways in which a group of people relate themselves to their world and to other groups and classes of people within it. In this respect learning and development is not located 'in the heads' of individuals, but *in the relationship* between social groups and their world.

Here language is seen as a site of struggle and contest. Dominant groups seek to limit and prescribe other groups' understanding of the world, to manage and marginalise other voices. But the campaigning/learning of other groups constantly stretches, tests and often punctures these limits. As this happens the group is confronted by contradictions between their own developing voices and the limits which have been prescribed. Working through these is often a difficult and complicated process, involving psychological friction and perhaps significant emotional pain. It is here that Freire believes that the development worker has a crucial role to play. It is as someone who assists the group to confront the contradictions which can block the development of their own voice. The worker seeks to identify these contradictions and present them back to the collective, as problems which require explanation and resolution. The idea is that in tackling these contradictions collectively the group themselves can clear the pathways of their own development. In this the worker is an active part of the process, but they do not prescribe its logic. The process has its own logic deriving from the relationship between the group and their world – a continually developing relationship in which language plays a crucial role.

As we explained earlier, we are attracted to these ideas because we feel that they speak clearly to our experience and practice in Lilybank (and elsewhere). However reading Freire is no talisman for the community worker. So how do we actually learn from his ideas in a way which might help us to reassert a radical agenda for community work practice ?

Changing minds: the role of word meaning

Here, we believe that the work of the psychologist Lev Vygotsky (1978, 1986.[4]) can help us to concretise some of what Freire is saying in

---

4. These works were written in the Soviet Union in the late 1920s and early 1930s. It is only since the 1960s and 1970s that they have been available in English, and only more recently that their significance for social psychology has been at all appreciated (Kozulin 1986, 1990; Van der Veer and Valsiner 1990; Wertsch 1985, 1991).

relation to language. This is no coincidence, for much of what Freire is saying is traceable to Vygotsky's influence.[5]

Vygotsky, like Freire, sees language as the key to the relationship between human beings and their world, the key to the human mind. Very briefly, his reasoning is as follows. In their pre-linguistic stages children can make sounds, and they can also think, but as yet they lack the capacity for intelligible speech. It is only when these two capabilities become 'internally connected' during socialisation that speech is possible. The internal connection is that of *word meaning*. When this connection is made vocalising involves thought, and thinking becomes verbalized (with inner speech). For Vygotsky this new connection transforms the whole structure of the mind, and makes the development of the 'higher mental functions' specific to the human species possible. Language becomes a focal point around which the mind is organized – a kind of 'strategic command centre' around which other functions (perception, memory, attention, imagination) revolve.

But the human mind is not a static *thing*. It is a continually developing *process*. So understanding it means understanding it *in its development*. Here Vygotsky is led to a view of the mind as a process in which gradual changes give way to ruptures and sudden shifts in which it is dramatically reorganised. It is learning which leads to these shifts, but language is also given a crucial role. Learning leads to changes in word meanings, which lead to a re-orientation of the mind as a whole. Linguistic change is *not* held to have *caused* the shift here. What Vygotsky *is* saying is that changes in word meaning signal the decisive moments in the learning process – the movement to a new 'mind-set'.

What we take from Vygotsky, then, is the need to focus on the way in which word meanings change. For us this is vital in trying to understand the learning process of groups with which we work. But how do word meanings change?

Word meaning: the dynamics of evaluation

The work of Valentin Volosinov, written in the late 1920s helps us to add a necessary third dimension to our picture (Volosinov 1986, Gardiner 1992). This is primarily because Volosinov is concerned

---

5. See comments made by V. John-Steiner and E. Souberman in their 'Afterword' to Vygotsky's Mind in Society.

with the way in which language develops through social conflict in capitalist societies. The parallel with Vygotsky is striking. As groups experience the social and economic development of their world they go through a learning process. This learning is seen to culminate in changes in the meanings of the words which the group use to talk about that world. As was the case for Vygotsky, this is seen to be an occasion of profound significance for the restructuring of the mind.

But, as we know from Freire, there is nothing automatic about this process in a society with systematic inequalities of power and wealth. Here the powerful seek to prescribe and limit the voice of the others, to impose their own words and meanings on them – often with significant success. The others are then left trying to find their own voice through the medium of the imposed voice of another. Volosinov offers us a simple, yet powerful way of grasping the dynamics of this difficult process.

Here the question of evaluation comes to the fore. Anything which is really important to the life of a group is subjected to their evaluation (see Volosinov 1986: 70). Whether explicitly or implicitly, whenever they speak about it they evaluate it from the point of view of the life of the group. The rub is that different groups with radically different points of view share a single language. Yet when they speak, their characteristic evaluations produce quite different meanings within the same words. The result is that the singular nature of the language can serve to mask the competing meanings which different groups realise when they speak. The power of dominant groups can be used to further reinforce this masking of diversity and conflict – by seeking to prevent the development of meanings antagonistic to their own, and by devaluing, ridiculing and marginalising hostile meanings where they do develop. Here language not only mediates the relationship between people and their world. Dominant powers seek to make it a *distorting medium* in the relationship.

However dominant power is not omnipotent. Dissent is always present in some form. In the worst case it will lie dormant. At other times it will rise to the surface and puncture the limits which dominant powers seek to impose. Then we find a polarisation within language as different groups realize antagonistic evaluations of the vital processes of social and economic change which are affecting their lives. In so doing they unmask the intentions concealed in the uses of language made by dominant groups. The same words are mobilized in different ways, with different meanings and intentions, by different speakers. Words come to embody 'the clash of live social accents'.

> Any current curse word can become a word of praise, any current truth must inevitably sound to many other people as the greatest lie. This ... quality of the [word] comes out fully in the open only in times of social crises ... In the ordinary conditions of life, the contradiction embedded in every [word] cannot emerge fully because [the word] in an established dominant ideology is always somewhat reactionary and tries, as it were, to stabilize ... the ... flux of the social generative process, so accentuating yesterday's truth as to make it appear today's. And that is what is responsible for the ... distorting peculiarity of the [word] within the dominant ideology. (Volosinov 1986: 23-24).

So what we are suggesting here is this: Freire tells us that language is simultaneously the site of a crucial political contest, and the key to understanding the psychology of learning which takes place as communities develop. If we accept this position – and it is difficult to conceive of a reasonable basis for rejecting it – then Vygotsky and Volosinov are clearly offering key insights as to how to build on it. What they are telling us is that the key way in which language develops is through changes in word meanings which emerge as groups polarise and clarify their own distinctive meanings through conflict. And in turn the key to this polarisation is the counter-evaluations which groups offer *within* the same words which they use to speak about their world. Moreover, we are suggesting that these insights are not simply theoretical, but also of clear practical value. Here we return to our experience and practice to demonstrate this.

Ferguslie Park: unmasking the language of 'partnership'

The general history of Ferguslie Park is well known to community development workers. It was a CDP area in the early 1970s and later it earned a significant reputation for assertive tenant organisation and activity in the Ferguslie League of Action Groups (FLAG) (Kintrea 1992; William Roe Associates 1994). By the early 1980s local government actually felt that they were losing control of the area as tenants responded aggressively to the local impact of Thatcherite policies of de-industrialization and cuts in local government finance. In the words of the local Regional Councillor:

> In the early eighties there had been quite a bit of, of eh, unrest in the area, there was large scale demonstrations in relation to rent rises and stuff like that [local authority demolition programme CC/JL] as Housing Support Grants were phased out. So relations between the local authorities and the community were very, very bad in the early eighties .(Interview with Harry Revie, 28/3/ 91).

The response of the local authorities was to grant Ferguslie Area Initiative status (1984-88) and to deploy community development techniques to co-opt the tenants to a strategy of limited investment and the management of continuing decline. The Initiative proved to be quite 'successful' in these terms (Ferguslie Park Strategy Group 1988).

> ... during that time, in fact, it was a deliberate strategy of Strathclyde that we try and encourage community participation with local government, and that members become involved in that process. Eh, I think we were very lucky in Ferguslie that two out of the three councillors ... were able to get ... very, very heavily involved with trying to restore the relations between the local authorities and the local community, and I think that, in truth, during that four year period, we did manage [that] (Interview with Harry Revie, 28/3/91).

This 'success' in turn provided some basis for yet another 'community development' initiative. In 1988 Ferguslie was designated by the Scottish Office as one of four 'Partnership' areas (Scottish Office 1988; 1989). The strategy in these areas was for central government to break the existing local authority led approach to urban problems – which, for them, reeked of 'dependency'. They would seek to encourage the private sector to provide a solution, while the Scottish Office itself co-ordinated the efforts of the local authorities, who were cast in an 'enabling role', and a range of other voluntary agencies and quangos. Local potential for property and business development would be harnessed to the task of 'renewal', and the area would be geared into the 'new realities' of the 1990s (See Collins 1991b). Everything was to be subordinated to this aim. This included 'community development', for the Scottish Office's objectives could only be achieved through careful management of a local population which had a fairly recent history of 'causing trouble'. For their part, the local authorities, gutted by the election of the third Thatcher Government, were largely willing to go along with this agenda. This was particularly true of Strathclyde who actually argued that the policy ideas forwarded by the Government had been developed by Strathclyde themselves (Strathclyde Regional Council 1988).

The rhetoric of 'partnership' was used to mask this agenda. And the fact that the local authorities publicly endorsed that rhetoric made it all the more difficult to unmask. To local people it was presented as an exercise in 'participation', 'local control' and even 'empowerment', of 'local people taking control back from bureaucrats and having a say in building a better future'. The 'partnership' spoke to them in a language which seemed to be 'their own', but which had in fact been taken from them and appropriated by the Scottish Office for quite different purposes. For a time this tactic paid off. But by the latter part of 1990 tenants began to express serious doubts as to what was really going on. A learning process was clearly under way, as tenants compared rhetoric with reality. At this point the tenants commissioned a researcher to examine their role in the Partnership. The idea was to provide a basis for them to mount a campaign for change. What emerged from the research was that their role in the process was purely legitimatory. 'Participation' and 'partnership' were simple euphemisms used to mask the unpleasant realities involved in securing the compliance of community organizations with an externally-imposed agenda designed, primarily, to free up land close to Scotland's largest airport (See Collins 1991a, 1992[6]; also Kintrea 1992).

But something of equal importance which emerged was the way in which their participation in the research project seemed to act as a 'catalyst' in their learning. This was a purely accidental finding, but it is one which Freire helps us to understand. It seemed that the

6. These papers are available from Chik Collins, University of Paisley, 0141-848-3892. The 1992 paper (What's This All About Then ? Tenant Participation in the Ferguslie Park 'Partnership') was written at the request of the Tenants' Information Service who subsequently decided not to publish it.

tenants' participation in the research led them to confront and to begin to resolve the contradictions which they experienced between their own voice and the imposed language of the Partnership. But this was no simple, 'logical' process – it was characterized by apprehension, fear and even dread. In private one-to-one interviews the tenants were, literally and metaphorically, looking over their shoulder as they developed their criticisms of the Partnership. Almost like dissidents in a totalitarian regime, they feared that 'dangerous talk' would have 'consequences'.

Still the tenants own voice clearly began to emerge, and it emerged through an unfolding battle over language – a battle over the *meaning of key words* (see Collins 1995). In Volosinov's terms, the key words in the language of 'partnership' were being relocated between 'evaluative contexts' – from that of the Scottish Office and its various 'partners' (including Strathclyde Regional Council) to the evaluative context of the tenants on the receiving end of the new strategy. As a result *word meanings changed*. Increasingly partnership itself became a dirty word. It was almost as if all the grievances which the tenants felt were distilled and signified in this one word. Words like 'participation' and 'consultation' would only be entertained if they were prefaced with the word 'real' to distinguish what the tenants meant from the duplicity of the Partnership. The mind-set was changing – and this was clearly signalled by the crucial linguistic changes in progress. This did not escape the notice of the Partnership. Tenants were beginning to talk about going back to campaigning on a range of issues, even of withdrawing from the Partnership as tenants had done in Castlemilk Partnership in 1990. This was precisely the scenario the Partnership had to avoid.

As the language polarised, the tenants were increasingly faced with a clear choice between their own voice and the ventriloquism of the Partnership. But it was a choice that the Partnership were not going to leave them free to make for themselves. Quite the reverse. The Partnership intervened directly through their own 'Community Development Executive' (CDE) – (himself a former activist who had become a significant figure in the local Labour Party) – and through the offices of the local Regional Councillor (Strathclyde Regional Council 1991). Their objective was to replace FLAG as the representative community organization with a new, specially created 'Community Forum'. In the interim, they sought to restructure FLAG by removing some groups and incorporating others so as to dilute, and ultimately remove, its critical edge. More immediately, leading activists were either removed from the organisation or 'induced' into agreeing to the restructuring process. In relation to the latter, the promise of paid positions for 'full-time activists' seems to have played a role (McIntyre 1991). In this situation some chose to capitulate. Others chose to go down battling. Here the fear and loathing referred to above begin to make sense. The prospect of FLAG facing down the Partnership was simply not on the agenda. But why ?

We believe that the explanation can only be provided by taking a long hard look at the work of the joint local authority Area Initiative and the way in which community work was deployed within it. The problem which the FLAG activists faced was that they were isolated – primarily *within* their own community, but also from *other* communities (especially the other 3 Partnership areas in Scotland). Yet in the early 1980s the situation had been rather different – especially in terms of the relationship between FLAG's leaders and the local population as a whole. Then FLAG was in a position to mobilize the community, and it was this threat which led the local authorities to set up the Area Initiative. This Initiative was used to change the nature of FLAG quite dramatically. It directed FLAG away from mobilising the community on a broad democratic basis, and towards a straightforward co-option to the management of decline. It has to be said that this was achieved despite the efforts of some community workers to assist the more assertive elements in the community to oppose it. But ultimately they too found themselves dragged along by the politics of their situation.

This was the beginning of the neutering of FLAG. It was a process which was later to lead to its effective liquidation, for the community development strategy of the Area Initiative had generated a type of community organisation which was not capable of handling the situation which emerged later in relation to the Partnership. Lacking the capacity to mobilise the community, FLAG were on a hiding to nothing – and a hiding was what they got. Subsequently the Scottish Office actually moved their own CDE into FLAG's premises to keep a closer eye on things. Since then FLAG has been replaced as the 'representative' organization of the local community by the new Community Forum – custom-built for the Partnership's purposes (Collins 1992; Kintrea 1992; William Roe Associates 1994). The Partnership's former CDE is now the Chief Executive of this Forum, and he supervises the work of former activists now employed through the Forum as Community Development Officers. And for daring to assist the more assertive elements in the local community to oppose all of this, Regional community development staff found that they were no longer required in Ferguslie Park.

More recently, the headlines which have emerged from Ferguslie Park would seem to project dire warnings for all those who are concerned with questions of urban policy, democracy and the impact of community development practices on the communities which they are (supposedly) intended to serve. The estate is at the centre of an alleged scandal surrounding the role of the local community business in relation to drug selling and money lending in the Paisley area. There is also alleged manipulation of the local Labour Party branch in political manoeuvring over re-selection of parliamentary candidates.[7] Yet, in the light of the recent history of the estate recounted above, these allegations might not seem altogether surprising. In general terms, if one sets out to neuter assertive social and democratic organizations, then one should not be surprised if anti-social and anti-democratic forces find the space they need to develop their influence.

Conclusion

The Ferguslie case study pulls the main threads of our argument together. In it we see clearly the process through which a community group progressively finds its own voice in the context of a campaign. We also see the crucial importance of language in this process. We see that, above all, the process involved the group comparing the rhetoric of 'partnership' with their actual experience. Word meanings played the key role here, and we can see that they changed as a result of the polarisation which developed as key words were relocated between 'evaluative contexts'. In short, if, with Freire, we want to understand more of the psychology of learning amongst groups as they campaign to assert more meaningful democratic control over the forces determining their lives, then the contributions of Vygotsky and Volosinov would seem to provide a starting point.

But what is also very significant is the way in which the group's involvement in the production of the report seemed to act as a 'catalyst' or 'lubricant' as they worked through the difficult process of developing their own 'evaluative accents' and finding their own voice.

7. For the headlines, and detailed coverage of these allegations, see *The Herald* and *The Scotsman* (esp. week beginning 17th April 1995) and *Scotland on Sunday* (esp. 16th, 23rd and 30th April 1995).

In the case of Ferguslie this was quite accidental. Yet it seems, to us, that for those who seek to reassert a more radical agenda for community work practice this accident may offer some significant pointers. Some of this perspective was introduced to tenants in Lilybank last year, and they used it quite self-consciously as a tool in dismantling the mechanisms by which they had been co-opted to the scheme of GDC, Scottish Homes and Parkhead Housing Association.

However this perspective also poses some rather difficult questions for community workers. For it demonstrates just how 'community development' can be deployed to diminish the ability of a community to sustain its own voice in the harsh socio-political climate of the 1990s (see also Player in this volume). Even more worrying is the fact that today we might well be told that the type of community work which accomplished this in the mid 1980s is now too radical! The problem posed is that campaigning work in the 1990s requires not simply the rejection of the 'new' model advocated by the 'new realists', but also the transcendence of the limits imposed on communities by the earlier model. As we said earlier, this is not a problem for the faint-hearted, or, for that matter, for the career-minded.

Of course, we are not suggesting in this paper that community workers should be taking up the study of esoteric elements of psychology for their own sake. What we are re-emphasising – with the help of some old ideas, some new ideas, and in the context of new socio-economic circumstances – is something which proponents of radical community work have always been aware of. This is, that the collectivization of local experiences of poverty, and the ability of the collective to sustain itself in a political contest, hinges to a very great extent on community groups developing and sustaining their own political voice, and not being divided and co-opted to the singing of someone else's tune. What we hope to have contributed in the paper is a critical perspective on some of the practices which have led to communities being deprived of the resources necessary to achieve this, and some theoretical and practical tools which might be of value to community workers who would seek to help those communities develop them in the present and future.[8]

8. The contents of this paper are derived from materials which were prepared for a training day on 'Campaigning and the Community Worker' with workers from the Glasgow (North West) Community Development Team of Strathclyde Regional Council (October 1994). The authors would like to thank the workers from the
(cont. on next page)

References

Barr, A. (1990). *Practising Community Development: Experience in Strathclyde*. London: CDF Publications

Barr, A. *et al* (1995). *Strong Communities, Effective Government: The Role of Community Work* (2 vols). Glasgow: Scottish Community Development Centre

Coates, D. (1979). *What Went Wrong ? Explaining the Fall of the Labour Government*. Nottingham: Spokesman

Coates, K. (1980). *Labour in Power? A study of the Labour Government 1974-79*. London: Longman

Collins, C. (1991a). *Community Participation in the Ferguslie Park Partnership: A Report to the Ferguslie League of Action Groups*. Paisley: FLAG

Collins, C. (1991b). Partnerships: what's it all about? *CIN (Newsletter of the Community Information Network)*. 1, pp. 2-5

Collins, C. (1992). What's This All About Then? Tenant Participation in the Ferguslie Park 'Partnership'. Unpublished manuscript

Collins, C. (1995). 'The Dialogics of 'Community': Struggle and Identity in a Scottish Working Class Housing Scheme'. Paper presented at conference on 'Ideas of Community', University of the West of England, 14th/15th September 1995. Available in Conference Proceedings

Craig, G. (1989). Community work and the state. *Community Development Journal*. 24, pp. 3-18

Cuthelton/Lilybank Tenants' Forum (1991-1995). *The Lilybank Lampost*

(cont.)
North West District for the opportunity to present our ideas to them, and for the contribution which they have made to their further development through their participation in the training. Thanks are due to John Foster and Erik Sutherland (University of Paisley) who offered useful comments on an earlier draft of this paper.

Ferguslie Park Strategy Group (1988). *Setting the Pattern: A Review of the Area Initiative, 1984-1988,* Paisley: Strathclyde Regional Council

Ferguson, I. (1992). Review of Barr (1991). *Critical Social Policy.* 34. pp. 119-124

Foster, J. and Woolfson, C. (1986). *The Politics of the UCS Work-In.* London: Lawrence and Wishart

Freire, P. (1972a). *The Pedagogy of the Oppressed.* Harmondsworth: Penguin

Freire, P. (1972b). *Cultural Action for Freedom.* Harmondsworth: Penguin

Gardiner, M. (1992). *The Dialogics of Critique: M. M. Bakhtin and the Theory of Ideology.* London: Routledge

Kintrea, K. (1992). Ferguslie Park Partnership. *In:* Alan McGregor, et al. *Community Participation in Areas of Urban Regeneration: A Report to Scottish Homes.* Edinburgh: Scottish Homes

Kozulin, A. (1986). Vygotsky in context. *In:* Lev S. Vygotsky. *Thought and Language,* London: MIT Press

Kozulin, A. (1990). *Vygotsky's Psychology: A Biography of Ideas.* London: Harvard University Press

Labour Party (1973). *Labour's Programme 1973.* London: Labour Party

Lister, Jim (written with AFTER Group) (1991). Community involvement in the Gear area. *In:* Maguiness, ed. *Housing, Industry and Community Development in the West of Scotland: The New Agendas.* Local Government Centre, Paisley College

McGregor, A. et al (1992). *Community Participation in Areas of Urban Regeneration: A Report to Scottish Homes* Edinburgh: Scottish Homes

McIntyre, J. (1991). 'FLAG Information', unpublished report on meetings to restructure FLAG, July–September

Scottish Office (1988). *New Life for Urban Scotland.* Edinburgh: HMSO

Scottish Office (1989). *A Pattern for New Life: Strategy for the Regeneration of Ferguslie Park.* Edinburgh: HMSO.

Strathclyde Regional Council (1983). *Social Strategy for the Eighties.* Glasgow: Strathclyde Regional Council

Strathclyde Regional Council (1984). *Helping the Community to Organize: Review of Community Work.* Glasgow: Strathclyde Regional Council

Strathclyde Regional Council (1988). *Generating Change – Urban Regeneration: The Strathclyde Experience.* Glasgow: Strathclyde Regional Council

Strathclyde Regional Council (1991). 'Analysis of Community Participation Within The Formal Structures of the Partnership', unpublished Council report

Van der Veer, R. and Valsiner, J. (1991). *Understanding Vygotsky: A Quest for Synthesis.* Oxford: Basil Blackwell

Volosinov, V. N. (1986). *Marxism and the Philosophy of Language.* London: Seminar Press

Vygotsky, L. S. (1986). *Thought and Language.* London: MIT Press

Vygotsky, L. S. (1978). *Mind in Society.* London: Harvard University Press

William Roe Associates (1994). *An Evaluation of Community Involvement in the Ferguslie Park Partnership.* Edinburgh: The Scottish Office Central Research Unit

Wertsch, J. (1985). *Vygotsky and the Social Formation of Mind.* London: Harvard University Press

Wertsch, J. (1991). *Voices of the Mind.* London: Harvester-Wheatsheaf

Chapter 3: Partnership or Incorporation?

John Player

Synopsis

This chapter focuses on the elements of continuity and change in British Urban Policy. The British State is in crisis, requiring the need to explore – perhaps rediscover – instruments of policy to manufacture the consent and manage the dissent of those disaffected and disadvantaged by the wider political economy. The competitive localism which characterises the Partnership process is part of the hegemonic restructuring of welfare within a 'free market' system. The author revisits the origins of community development, in both colonial and domestic contexts, identifying the continuity of economic, political and ideological purposes.

Whilst recognising the continuity of the contradictory positions of those who work within the state apparatus, he argues for the development of a counter-hegemonic opposition as the only way of strengthening working class interests against those of the market. The politics of Partnerships may in this sense offer potential for the development of critical participation aimed at social change.

Introduction

'The Time is out of joint': by way of a theoretical forethought it is curious at this point in time that the arch de-constructionist, Jaques Derrida (1994), should be quoting Hamlet as a backdrop to plea for the resurrection of Marx. The fact that Derrida is expressing a feeling of solidarity with a certain spirit of Marx, thereby 'promising' a critique of the concepts of state and nation, shows a degree of courage at this moment in European history. It is, according to Ahmad (1994), an affirmative gesture in the face of all contrary winds

It is to this certain spirit of Marx that we might look to enable us to gain an insight into the role of the state in relation to the poverty experiments – a 'spectre' which we might resurrect to throw some light on the relationship between the uneven development of capitalism and the development of national and local institutions which manage dissent and manufacture consent – a spirit that might come to 'haunt' the barbarism that threatens and poisons human survival. One of the tenets of this spectre, is that central to the process of capitalist production and reproduction, is the notion of uneven development in space and time. Marx's aphorism was that capitalism perpetually strives to annihilate space and time and Derrida suggests that the time is out of joint.

Space and time

The spaces in time I am considering here are the four Scottish Office-led Partnerships with particular emphasis on the Wester Hailes Partnership in Edinburgh. As a Community Development Worker employed by Lothian Regional Council's Community Education Service (CES) in Wester Hailes, this discussion gives me an opportunity to develop some themes and ideas based in part on empirical observation, having returned to Wester Hailes after ten years and, hopefully, open an ongoing dialogue with other workers and activists, especially in the other Partnership areas. I feel that such a dialogue would go some of the way to challenging the tendency in British urban policy to concentrate on neighbourhood to the detriment of the wider context of relative economic decline, retrogressive social policy and the archaic and undemocratic nature of the British State.

The British State is itself a multi-dimensional phenomenon, the nature of which varies across time and space. As with the key word 'community', the term 'partnership' has already acquired euphoric connotations evoking uncritical feelings of warmth and belonging (see Collins and Lister in this volume). By deconstructing the 'apple-pie' notion of Partnership we might begin to examine the hierarchical nature of the British State's stretch across territory. Moreover, it presents an opportunity to explore the state as a social relation and a chance to grapple with and theorize power itself.

The community solution – past and present

Some 'spectres' and haunting spirits to be considered when looking at the initiatives arising out of 'New Life For Urban Scotland' (1988) must be the parallels with the Home Office Community Development Projects (CDPs) established in 1968. For, as Turock (1994) points out, a key feature of British urban policy is its consistent emphasis on small areas. This area-based approach entailed the targeting of policies and resources into areas with the express aim of combating the problems therein. Underpinning such initiatives is a social pathology approach to the problems of continuing poverty and multiple deprivation. Spatially-based strategies, then, are advocated by policy makers to address what is considered to be a peripheral problem of the spatial concentration of poverty. This approach, echoed in the Partnership initiatives, has been succinctly described by Massey (1994) as 'geographically blaming the victim'. Moreover, Robinson (1994) argues that it is illusory to suggest that spatially targeted urban policy alone will solve urban problems.

The CDP reports were suffused with this argument. A rereading of such reports as 'The Costs of Industrial Change' (1977), 'Permanent Unemployment' (1978), 'In and Out of Work' (1978) and 'Gilding the Ghetto' (1977) make for uncanny reading indeed. If the literary theorist, Derrida, is arguing that we would do well to re-read the 'Communist Manifesto' and 'Capital', perhaps now is the time to read again and discuss the CDP reports. Theoretically the CDP workers left us with the legacy of a Marxist analysis rooted in notions of uneven development and neo-colonialism. Whilst many pertinent criticisms of this particular paradigm have been made, especially in relation to the need for a class perspective to be articulated with gender and race, it is very difficult not to be moved by the clarity and 'bottle' inherent in these reports.

The British State learnt its own lessons from the CDP projects and effectively closed them down. Community development initiatives funded by the Home Office were subsequently encouraged to adopt the more pluralistic and neighbourhood focused perspective represented in the works of Thomas (1976). This perspective is evident in the Partnership approach and a sort of 'pluralistic pragmatism' pervades the whole process. However, this approach suffers from a weakness that is intrinsic in pluralism itself in that it fails to explain the structural origins of power. Moreover, these shortcomings are compounded by the nature of the forces which have created urban decline and the context within which urban regeneration occurs.

The short-termism of the quick fix of immediate resources to ameliorate the problem of poverty is obviously part of the Partnership's appeal. In fact the promise of resources, money and power has been the attraction and the mechanism for securing the consent of local people. It is perhaps not by accident that the areas of Wester Hailes and Castlemilk (in Glasgow) were chosen by the Scottish Office in 'New Life for Urban Scotland' (1988) with their histories of community action and dissent. McArthur (1993), when discussing participation in Partnerships, highlights the situation in one of the Partnership initiatives where the community representatives were drawn from a mature community organisation representing a well-developed network of tenants' associations covering the whole of the housing estate: this organisation had developed a reputation as a body prepared to challenge authority, with a track record of effective campaigning and street protest. He goes on to argue, however, that this is no longer the case and refers to Mcgregor et al (1995) who maintain that this organisation has become incorporated into the bureaucratic machinery of the Partnership.

This notion of incorporation is a criticism articulated by workers and activists in both Wester Hailes and Castlemilk. Partial consent is secured by allowing the 'community' the dominant influence in the dedicated Urban Programme budget. In Wester Hailes this amounts to two and a half million pounds a year. Not only does this create what has been described as a 'consultative elite', but also mirrors the coherent strategy of self-representation adopted by the British in India before Independence. The creation of participative structures was a key function of colonial community development, which was to have an influence on British community work policy and practice. As Mayo (1975) points out, one of the consequences of British colonial policy was the introduction of the Indian community development programme prior to independence in 1947. This whole programme, according to Mayo, was 'an attempt to create plausibly democratic institutions without serious dislocation to the vested interests of the status quo'. Gramsci (1926) was also anxious to point out that 'colonisation' was not only international but also domestic. One of the lessons from Gramsci, according to Viswanathan (1992), in his 'English Literary Study in British India', is that cultural domination operates by consent. I would argue that one of the domestic instruments for securing consent is through the 'moral and intellectual suasion' of Partnership.

Local people are not simply duped by such programmes but are faced with the dilemma outlined by McArthur (1993) of 'whether to participate or to remain in conflict with authority'. Moran (1995) maintains that the 'community' in Wester Hailes is far from 'zipped up the back' and contends that, because of firm community involvement in the Partnership process, the Scottish Office was unable 'to get away with' large scale privatisation of the housing stock.

As Dymond (1994) has also pointed out, participation in the Partnership process in Wester Hailes has led to gains in the field of housing with the demolition of unpopular high rise blocks and the creation of terraced and semi detached housing. Moreover, Dymond stresses that the 'community' was successful in resisting the full extent of tenure changes to promote owner occupation proposed by Scottish Homes – the national housing agency – in the housing sub group of the Partnership. It remains unclear, however, the extent to which these housing gains made in Wester Hailes have been at the expense of tenants in other areas of Edinburgh. It is difficult to secure information from Edinburgh District Council Housing Department which would determine whether or not Partnership status in Wester Hailes and the resulting increased investment has been at the expense of housing projects in other areas.

It has, nevertheless, been argued that much of the housing improvements, apart from housing renovations, in Castlemilk are not for existing residents. It would appear that on the issue of housing the 'community' agenda has been transformed to suit the agenda of the Government (see Doyle et al in this volume). Patterson (1995) refers to the recent evaluation report, carried out by the School for Advanced Urban Studies (SAUS, 1995), arguing that Castlemilk is being 'gentrified' in order to meet employment and incomes targets. His argument is that the population in Castlemilk is falling partly because of a housing policy that denies public sector housing to Castlemilk people even if they present themselves as homeless and have local connections. Effectively, the housing waiting list in Castlemilk is closed. Patterson is expressing a concern that the agenda of the major sponsors is about testing methods for the restructuring of housing markets that will result in a further residualisation of the more vulnerable and the poor. This will be compounded if levels of housing investment are dramatically reduced once the Partnership exits, creating obvious tensions between residents of 'improved' and 'unimproved' houses.

Partnerships and the market – privatising poverty

This process of testing out methods for the restructuring of housing markets is taking place in conjunction with an ongoing restructuring of the labour market. The increasing casualisation of the labour force with a persistent pool of long term unemployed and a peripheral workforce of part-timers, temporary workers and the self-employed is well documented elsewhere. What the recent SAUS evaluation report of Castlemilk Partnership suggests is the manner in which the two processes are interconnected; that, whilst measured on the basis of official figures, unemployment in Castlemilk has fallen towards the Glasgow average, Castlemilk has been a net exporter of the unemployed. The SAUS report argues that the shifting population structure consequent upon housing change may be as significant an influence on employment and unemployment in Castlemilk as labour market and job creation measures; that area based approaches without the development of an overarching framework for urban policy amounts to moving the problem elsewhere.

Those people who remain in the Partnership areas such as Wester Hailes can expect, according to recent local job centre figures, to be employed on a temporary basis on a wage level considered by any recognised definition as low, in a service sector industry, most probably hotel and catering. Low pay is argued to be one of the major causes of poverty and it highlights the paradox again of the area based approach to urban policy. On the one hand Central Government abolished the wages councils, designed to protect those vulnerable to abuse by employers whilst, on the other, attempting to ameliorate the consequences of poverty through small-scale, locally-based initiatives. Robinson (1994) argues that the first step to developing any meaningful urban policy should involve a return to the idea first outlined over fifty years ago in the 1944 White Paper on Employment: government commitment to pursuing the goal of full employment with the added caveat of a national minimum wage.

Returning to the significance of 'time' and 'space' these paradoxes, already touched upon, were inherent in the introduction of the four Partnership areas in 1989. The setting up of these initiatives came in the wake of the introduction of the Social Fund which was the result of a complete overhauling of the means-tested welfare benefits system. Single payments were abolished altogether and the Discretionary Social Fund was introduced in 1988. In fact as Townsend (1993) recently pointed out, in the Thatcher years there were more than thirty changes in the structure of Social Security which had the effect of reducing total state outlay to the poor. This included a freeze on the purchasing value of state pensions, the abolition of earnings-related benefits and a reduction in the scope and value of unemployment benefits, especially for people under 25 years of age. This restructuring of social policy against the poor came at a time when, as Mooney (1994) argues, Government urban policy was influenced by notions of 'targeting', reflected in such initiatives as Task Forces, City Challenge and 'New Life for Urban Scotland'.

The underlying economic philosophy in this period was 'trickle down'; the idea that, once generated, economic prosperity would filter through to the more disadvantaged groups in society. Conservative urban policy clearly gave increased prominence to the role of the private sector. 'New life for Urban Scotland' is suffused with such a philosophy, urging the private sector to take the lead in urban regeneration. This rhetoric now seems misguided to say the least. The reality is that it is, in fact, difficult to discern any private sector input into the Partnership strategies (see Mcgregor et al, 1995). Perhaps, more importantly, we have witnessed what Cochrane (1993) has described as a revolutionary change in the assumptions underlying the welfare state and this has been achieved not with a bang of legislation but through the whimper of Partnership. This is, perhaps, exemplified by local initiatives such as the Baby Item Borrowing Scheme (BIBS) set up by the Partnership Resource Team in Wester Hailes to loan buggies and cots to local people which could be seen as connected to the abolition in 1987 of the Maternity Grant and Single Payments amounting to £187.45 for baby items. In Wester Hailes, between 1988 and 1994, the proportion of households in receipt of benefit rose from 68% to 74% (McGregor er al, 1995) continuing to make this an ideal arena for Government experiments in area-based approaches to restructuring the Welfare State.

Cochrane (1993) and Wilks (1995) suggest that, since advanced capitalism apparently no longer needs the state to ensure that the entire labour force is housed, healthy and educated, the role of the welfare state is being fundamentally redefined. Their proposition is also that, in the absence of a public overhaul of the welfare state, the inner cities in England and the peripheral estates in Scotland are once again the site of new experiments, based on the redefinition of the social pathology diagnosis of urban policy – 'The time is out of joint' (Derrida, 1994).

The time is out of joint

Marxist critics differ in their prognosis for the welfare state with some arguing that it remains an enduring and irreversible institution of advanced capitalist countries. On the other hand some neo-Marxists, such as Offe (1982), now argue that what will follow is a minimalist welfare state for the poor, as the well-paid and affluent groups are encouraged into private insurance programmes. Offe is convinced that this 'residualisation' of welfare is due to the economic, industrial and employment changes of recent years that have led to a 'virtual evaporation' of classes and other groups who were the main supporters of collectivist values and the welfare state.

These collectivist values and assumptions, which underpinned the Keynsian welfare state, designed in part by Beveridge, included the principles of universality, of full male employment and of means-tested benefits becoming a residual element in the social security system. Whilst these assumptions have been contested by the New Right and the women's movement in particular (see Shaw, Meagher and Tett in this volume), what Cochrane (1993) is arguing is that the emphasis on competitive localism in urban policy and what Craig (1995) describes as the lottery of the Social Fund in social policy have contributed to a structural change in the welfare state. Cochrane, in his critique of Government led partnerships, maintains that some traditional welfare concerns such as urban deprivation are being simply reinterpreted as problems of economic growth so that urban regeneration is redefined as business confidence and new construction. He argues that a stress on development rather than welfare becomes dominant in the discourse surrounding partnerships with the more or less explicit assumption that urban regeneration through development will also improve matters for those who might otherwise have been recipients of welfare. What this means on the ground is, as Colenutt and Cutten point out (1994), that large amounts of public funds go to the private sector to bring forward these 'developments' and the community fail to secure any significant benefits.

Essentially Cochrane (1993) and others are putting forward the proposition that a structural change has taken place in the welfare state in that the characteristics of the post-war settlement with its recognition of the role of the working class and its organisations has given way to a new settlement in the 1980s arising from the crisis of social democracy in the 1970s which starts with the needs of business and its organisations. In that sense it is possible, according to Cochrane (1993) to identify a move from the welfare state to an enterprise state.

Nevertheless, due to the uneven development of capitalism and the peculiarities of the British State in Scotland it would seem sensible to be tentative about such claims of structural change. Cochrane's analysis focuses on the private sector and state relations in England and, whilst the Scottish Office have attempted to import a model of partnership from England, there remains in Scotland a different spatial fix. The inner-city areas in England offer development opportunities for the private sector (for example prime land), which the peripheral estates in Scotland on the whole do not. This is consistent with the structural dynamic of capital seeking out new markets at home and abroad. The Scottish Office has nevertheless, according to Craig (1995) in a recent discussion with activists in Wester Hailes, an agenda which 'is very much about increasing the low wage economy and selling council houses'. This critical view of Scottish Office led partnerships contrasts significantly with the numerous Labourist politicians who defer to Scottish Office endeavours at, what Robinson (1994) describes as, 'programme overkill in a strategic vacuum'.

Community work and partnerships – in a strategic vacuum

In an attempt to bring some of these disparate themes and concepts together it might be worth looking at the implications for community work practice, particularly since the perceived 'success' of the Scottish Office-led Partnerships is leading to the creation of similar approaches elsewhere. The recent proposal by the Scottish Office, 'Programme for Partnership' (1995), with its emphasis on 'Priority Partnership Areas' is an endeavour to encourage the formation of council-wide partnerships. Again, this urban policy instrument seems to be suffused with the notions of competitive localism inherent in City Challenge and Single Regeneration Budgets (SRB) urban funds. Given that community workers will increasingly find themselves employed in Partnerships Initiatives or in Partnership areas, we might do well to heed Bob Colenutt's (1995) comment that he 'doesn't think Partnership is a strategy'. Certainly the problems of deprivation and poverty which prompted the Scottish Office to devise special urban policy instruments still exist and in most of the urban priority areas the problems of unemployment, poverty, crime, physical decay, and poor housing have become significantly worse. Erskine (1995) highlights what he sees as a myth surrounding Partnerships – the partners are drawn together by common values and interests as much as by any specific gain. The reality is that the use of the term 'partnership' is one which conceals conflict. He argues that, where conflict is assumed not to exist, the status quo is preserved by ensuring that negotiated outcomes based upon a recognition of differing interests and power does not occur.

Perhaps community work should engage itself in 'Partnership free issues' (see Colenut, 1995) – supporting oppositional action in a more coherent manner. Community work is well placed to make a concerted effort to challenge the construct of competitive localism which passes for urban policy and practice. Community work might be enhanced if it paid attention to Bob Holman's (1993) emphasis on mutuality and cooperation, principles deeply rooted in working class social history. However, collective self-help such as food co-ops and Credit Unions have the potential for counter hegemonic opposition only if linked to a curriculum which includes political education and the practices of consumer boycott, direct action and the promotion of anti-capitalist social relations.

Critical participation

Along with the rebuilding of the autonomous base there is nevertheless, the need for critical participation in Scottish Office-led initiatives. This would, it seems to me, require serious discussion about strategy; strategy which understood the notion of 'in and against the State' and the Gramscian idea of 'war of position' (see Gramsci, 1971). The London-Edinburgh Weekend Return Group (L.E.W.R.G., 1979) publication 'In Against the State' pointed to the need for a strategy which took into account the contradiction of defending the welfare state against cutbacks whilst recognizing the need to go beyond a defence of the welfare state: 'to limit our actions to demands for 'more of the same' is to fail to take the opportunity to challenge capitalism fundamentally by rejecting its agenda, its definitions, its social relations'. This debate may become more difficult to facilitate with the rise of, what Cochrane (1993) sees as a management culture in the voluntary and statutory sectors with its deference to the 'neutral' techniques of the market. Nevertheless, community workers and radical practitioners in particular have an educational responsibility to assist local people to sharpen and clarify their understanding of the British State which, as Jessop (in McGregor et al, 1993) would have it, may be described as

'a strategically selective terrain which can never be neutral among all social forces and political projects;

but any bias is always tendentious and can be undermined or reinforced by appropriate strategies. For within the strategically selective limits established by state structures and operating procedures, the outcome of state power depends on the changing balance of forces engaged in political action both within and beyond the state'.

With Jessop's description in mind, I would like to conclude by proposing that a genuine 'community empowerment' strategy means the strengthening of working class interests against the market, the trick being to transform the state apparatus, not merely to bypass it (see Mayo, 1995). This strategy rests upon the increased and active intervention of mass community-based organisations in the state accompanied by the development of new forms of direct democracy and the flowering of self management networks and centres (see Poulantzas, 1980). The policies of local authorities must go further than the devolution of power to local neighbourhoods or area service committees. Local Authorities who see their role as protecting the interests of working class people need to address, along with local people, the real issue. How does community development and decentralisation relate to the fundamental redistribution of power and wealth? A lateral starting point might be a popular educational enquiry into the social pathology of control centres such as dominant financial institutions, the largest few hundred major trans-nationals which control the British economy, and the City of London!.

References

Ahmad, A. (1994). Response to Derrida. *New Left Review.* 208

Benwell Community Project, Final Report Series No. 2 (1978). *Permanent Unemployment.* Nottingham: The Russell Press Ltd

Brennan, T. (1989). Cosmopolitan and celebrities. *Race and Class.* 31(1)

CDP Inter-Project Editorial Team (1977). *The Costs of Industrial Change.* Newcastle Upon Tyne: CDP Publications

CDP Inter-Project Editorial Team (1977). *Gilding the Ghetto.* London: Tavistock Place

Cochrane, A. (1993). *Whatever Happened to Local Government.* Buckingham: Open University Press

Colenut, B. (1995). 'The Turn to Economic Development' discussion / workshop presentation to the 'Rivers of Blood: Cities in Crisis?' Conference 4th April 1995. University of Durham

Colenutt, B. and Cutten, A. (1994). Community empowerment in vogue or vain. *Local Economy.* 9(3), November

Craig, G. (1995). A Report on the Conference 'Wester Hailes against Poverty' held in Wester Hailes Representative Council, Lothian Regional Council Community Education Service

Derrida, J. (1994). *Specters of Marx.* New York: Routledge

Dymond, M. (1994). from interview with Dymond, Wester Hailes Representative Council, 3/11/1994

Erskine, A. (1995). 'Partnership: Another Urban Myth?' Paper presented to the 'Rivers of Blood: Cities in Crisis?' Conference 4th April 1995. University of Durham

Gramsci (1926). Some aspects of the southern question. *In:* Quintin Hoare, trans. and ed. *Selections from Political Writings 1921- 1926.* London: Lawrence and Wishart, 1978

Holman, B. (1993). *A New Deal for Social Welfare.* London: Lion Publishing

Industry Department for Scotland (1988). *New Life for Urban Scotland.* HMSO Dd. 812301 3/88 BP Ltd

London-Edinburgh Weekend Return Group (1979). *In and Against the State.* London: Pluto Press

McArthur, A. A. (1993). Community partnership: a formula for neighbourhood regeneration in the 1990s. *Community Development Journal.* 28(4), October

McGregor, A. et al. (1995). 'Interim Evaluation of Wester Hailes Partnership. Research Report' Centre for Housing Research and Urban Studies, University of Glasgow

Massey, D. (1994). *Space, Place and Gender.* Polity Press

Mayo, M. (1975). Community development, a radical alternative? *In:* Baily and Brake, eds. *Radical Social Work.* London: Arnold

Mayo, M. (1995). 'The Origins of Inner City Policy: and UK Cities since 1968. Some International Aspects of Community Participation.' Paper presented to the 'Rivers of Blood : Cities in Crisis' Conference, University of Durham 3/4 April 1995

Mooney, G. (1994). Review of Moon and Atkinson's *Urban Policy in Great Britain. Critical Social Policy No. 41*

Moran, J. (1995). A Report on the Conference 'Wester Hailes against Poverty' held in Wester Hailes Representative Council, Lothian Regional Council Community Education Service

North Tyneside CDP (1978). *In and Out of Work.* Nottingham: The Russell Press Ltd

Offe, C. (1982). Some contradictions of the modern welfare state. *Critical Social Policy.* 2(2)

Patterson, R. (1995). From interview with Patterson, 'Partnership Report 24/7/95' Lothian Regional Council Community Education Service

Poulantzas, N. (1980). *State, Power, Socialism.* London: Verso

Robinson, F. (1994). Urban policy under the Conservatives: in search of the Big Idea? *Local Economy.* 9, November

School for Advanced Urban Studies (1995). *The Castlemilk Partnership, Executive Summary.* University of Bristol

Scottish Office (1995). *Programme for Partnership.* HMSO

Thomas, D. N. (1976). *Organising for Social Change – A Study in the Theory and Practice of Community Work.* London: Allen and Unwin

Townsend, P. (1993). *The International Analysis of Poverty.* Hemel Hempstead: Harvester Wheatsheaf

Turock, I. (1994). Continuity, Change and Contradiction in Urban Policy. *Local Economy.* 9(3) November

Viswanathan, G. (1992). The beginnings of English literary study in British India. *In:* Donald and Rattansi. eds. *Race, Culture and Difference.* London: Sage

Wilks, S. (1995). 'Urban Experiments Limited Revisited: Urban Policy Comes Full Circle?' Paper presented to the 'Rivers of Blood: Cities in Crisis?' Workshop Conference, University of Durham, 3/4 April 1995

Chapter 4: Campaigning and Community Work

Mike Rosendale

Synopsis

In the summer of 1993 Tommy Sheridan, leading Scottish political and community activist, was asked by the 'Concept' journal to address an audience of community workers on the topic of 'Campaigning and Social Change'. Having developed an analysis of the limits of social change through democratic procedures in an increasingly undemocratic polity, Sheridan argued that it was only through civil disobedience – willingness to break the law – that the disaffected could make any significant gains in challenging a government whose purpose was to legislate people's services, rights and possibilities for legitimate resistance out of existence. His reference point for much of the discussion was the highly effective Anti-Poll Tax Campaign in Scotland. Whilst recognising the contradictory position of community workers employed by the state in supporting overtly political action, he also identified ways in which strategic, competent and democratic community work approaches could enhance the capacity of local people to undertake action for social change.

In this chapter, Mike Rosendale, a participant at the Concept Seminar, develops Sheridan's assessment of the potential for community work to operate in support of political action. The logic of the professional role of the community worker is to support people in identifying and challenging the root causes of their poverty or social exclusion. By emphasising the socio-political context within which learning takes place, he argues that it is not only legitimate for community workers to engage with groups struggling to improve their conditions but it is also an essential aspect of any educational practice committed to social justice. By examining how perceived organisational constraints can be challenged, he offers some practical insights for progressive practice.

Introduction

At the Concept seminar on 'Campaigning and social Change', in 1993, an audience of community workers and students gave Tommy Sheridan a rapturous welcome. The response to his speech was the closest I've seen to a standing ovation in 20 years of attending seminars and conferences.

Sheridan explained in his opening remarks that he was not used to this kind of event – his speeches were normally agitational in nature. Whether intentional or not, he certainly agitated most of his listeners. This is not surprising given that, whilst most of us present would identify ourselves with the so-called radical tradition in community work, most of his contribution was based on the experience of the anti- poll tax campaign – possibly the biggest single political issue to face Scottish people since the war – and yet one in which virtually no community workers, radical or otherwise, played any significant role! Perhaps the resounding applause for the speech was provoked by relief that he had not taken the opportunity to castigate and shame us. In fact, he was very encouraging; choosing to present the problem of a radical strand within the local state as a continuing challenge to our commitment, rather than writing us off as pseudo revolutionary windbags.

Campaigning and conflict

The cornerstone of his argument was that civil disobedience (breaking the law) will increasingly become a central component of effective mass campaigning. If we accept his analysis that opportunities to challenge decisions democratically have been so severely reduced in the past fifteen years, that there is no other alternative but passive acceptance, then we need to consider the implications for our practice.

Just in case we were tempted to resort to the argument that the geographically localised nature of most community work militates against such mass action, Sheridan talked about his involvement in a road safety campaign in Pollock. The campaign was successful in changing a bus route, and he identified clearly the key elements in its success: the issue was immediate and of great concern to local people; the chosen action involved many people acting together; it embarrassed the local political establishment, and the mass blocking of the road sounded like good fun. He linked that action to the creation of an unemployed workers' group looking at other political topics. The success of the road blockage inspired those involved to do more – "a wee sniff of victory encourages people." This unemployed group took up the poll tax issue in 1987, and the rest of the story, as they say, is history.

Sheridan acknowledged the difficulties faced by local authority community workers during the anti poll tax campaign, but also expressed a view widely held by local people – "Community workers are surely supposed to help local people with practical assistance". His advice to us was to 'box clever' on the basis that the Tory government was engaged in a long term legislative attack on the fabric of communities, which would also ultimately attack our jobs. He underlined the importance of building alliances, with trades unions, with local groups and management committees.

The discussion which followed was largely preoccupied with the dilemmas of 'political' community work, and the relationship between political and community activists. A memorable question came from one activist who wondered what community workers were for if they could not support 'political' campaigns? Given that the vast majority of community workers in my experience appear not to, then the question takes on major significance.

Direct action: the educative role

The dilemmas articulated by Tommy Sheridan should be examined in order that community workers, who consider themselves to be radical, can begin to arrive at some explanations for our apparent inability to match action with words during the last ten years. This raises questions about the nature of our role in supporting autonomous groups pursuing their collective interests. Our educational purpose remains the key to our relationship with groups who wish to pursue strategic direct action. So why don't community workers support 'political' campaigns? And what are they doing instead? This raises questions, firstly, about the purposes of community work and, secondly, about what constitutes a 'political' campaign.

It could be argued that the term 'community worker' is a generic one which is as helpful in defining purpose as is the term 'office worker'. It tells us where they work, but it certainly does not tell us what they do. Focusing on my sphere of experience, the local authority Community Education Service (CES), we can see that workers are engaged in a wide range of activities, mostly concerned with the management of delivering valuable local services. A minority of staff, however, have job remits which actively encourage them to work with people in a way which constitutes 'political' education. In my view the introduction and development of educational work in campaigning is the principal responsibility of community workers, and the professional justification for their involvement.

Of course many of my colleagues would dispute this view, arguing that community development, as defined in documents produced by the CES throughout Scotland, is an underpinning approach to all the work we do, and therefore that its use in a variety of settings has equal value in terms of educational potential. If we accept this view, then we can stop berating ourselves about our failure to engage in a radical agenda, because almost all CES workers can claim to have some involvement with groups of people acting to improve services in their localities. The problem is, however, that these issues are usually related directly to community education services, rarely moving beyond narrow interests to engage with more broadly relevant areas of social and economic activity; for example, the Community Centre Management Committee which pressurises officials and councillors for resources to open another youth club; the parents and toddlers' group which organises a deputation to the local council demanding more money for after school care, or teenagers who go to the press about the absence of skateboarding facilities.

Could the community workers who support these activities be said to be supporting political campaigns? If politics is "any activity concerned with the acquisition of power, or gaining one's own ends" (Collins English Dictionary 1991), then clearly these activities are political. Are they campaigns? Again, it could be argued that they are, because they usually include a series of coordinated activities aimed at achieving a particular goal.

So the conclusion, certainly with reference to the Community Education Service, is that a significant number of workers are already engaged in supporting political campaigns, albeit in areas of policy often defined by the priorities of the CES itself. It is also often the case that the pressure and the tactics employed are determined by the worker (consciously or otherwise); for example, if she or he can persuade management to fund a new club, then other tactics, which may have more of the appearance of 'campaigning' may not be necessary. This kind of approach, I would argue, whilst often getting results, takes away much of the potential for political education, begging the question: is a satisfactory result more important than engagement in a political process? If it is not, community workers may be accused of delaying the provision of badly-needed services in order to encourage the political development of a minority of local people. I would argue that the dichotomy between process and product, however, is a false one since the ability to engage in campaigning around collective interests is also more effective, in the long term, in challenging those inequalities which determine distribution of resources.

Often, a 'campaign' will emerge when the 'normal channels' fail. In this case, local groups going to the press, submitting petitions or lobbying councillors, are some of the tactics employed by community workers to gain more resources. Again, this may work in the short term, but the complex game of collusion between councillors, local people, face to face workers and senior officials, may mask the real causes of inequality and exclusion, preventing local activists from exploring, understanding and challenging those causes.

In order to move beyond the narrow range of issues normally addressed with community education support, workers need to create more time to spend away from service delivery and its management; we also need to engage in discussion with people without the constraint of professional censorship of priorities. By way of illustration, let us consider the issues of childcare and unemployment.

Many parents of young children want to work for a variety of reasons not least of which is to increase household income. However, they are often prevented from doing so by a range of factors such as lack of qualifications, lack of jobs, lack of confidence, lack of childcare. The increasing trend in recent years has been to focus on overcoming individual barriers through training and addressing childcare shortage by initiatives like the Lothian and Edinburgh Enterprise Limited (LEEL) After School Care scheme, established in collaboration with the CES In this way the 'problem' is located with the individual or with the neighbourhood's lack of facilities. Whilst it may be true that many individuals will gain from training, and some may even get a job, the majority, however, will not. It is also true that the acquisition of childcare facilities, is of great benefit to parents in that locality (see Findlay in this volume). However, the concentration of effort in solving 'problems' at the individual or neighbourhood level diverts attention from the wider political and economic causes.

This short-termism is also reflected in the development of the multi-agency partnership approach to improving areas of deprivation.

These initiatives are also characterised by a focus on the individual and the neighbourhood (see Player, Collins and Lister in this volume), and by an underlying view that concerted action at local level can solve all of these 'problems'. The evidence, of course, suggests otherwise, and perhaps the assertion by Gary Craig, speaking at a local seminar, that government-led partnerships are introduced to expand the low wage economy and sell off council houses, is closer to the truth.

It is certainly difficult for community workers to move beyond the parameters placed on the culture of activism in any one neighbourhood. For example, to work with groups exploring and acting politically on an issue such as unemployment would probably be regarded as self-indulgent and irrelevant in an area in which the norm is to pursue pragmatic solutions. Inevitably, community workers are influenced by the dominant culture and often become its key proponents – not necessarily by advocating it, but by submission to the apolitical route.

Professionalism, competence and credibility

There is, indeed, an issue of professionalism here. Community workers have a responsibility to support people in identifying and challenging the root causes of their poverty or social exclusion. That responsibility is not discharged professionally if the worker adopts a stance which precludes some issues or particular means of challenging their causes. A professional worker should support groups in considering all the options open to them. In a very real sense, this is the curriculum of community work, and the worker who censors that curriculum is acting unprofessionally. This comprehensive approach to the identification and exploration of issues should continue into the decision making process about tactics. If the group chooses to campaign then the question of direct action, raised by Sheridan, may well come into play when the limits of democratic protest have been reached. To deal with this, we need to focus on the role of the community worker.

Firstly, who defines the role? Technically the employer, reflecting broad professional definitions determines the role, which is translated into a job description. In practice, however, there is an area of negotiation between the official job description and its practical application, which hinges on professional interpretation. Added to this, the terminology which constitutes the professional discourse e.g.

empowerment, participation and relevance, is sufficiently ambiguous as to be able to support a range of purposes.

In the CES the worker's role is defined as primarily educational; but anyone who has tried to adopt that role in the midst of community action knows that they need more than their employer's approval to succeed. There is a key issue of credibility. Sheridan's view that "community workers are supposed to help local people with *practical* assistance" (my emphasis) is very important, and it is not just about being a handy resource. It is about solidarity. Educational opportunities abound during a campaign and a skilled worker can combine practical assistance and education in a way which makes a unique contribution to the immediate success of the action and to the longer term development of the group and its individual members in terms of political awareness (see Cooke in this volume). In my experience, a narrow interpretation of the educational role may hinder, or even undermine this potential. For many groups, the provision of practical assistance is crucial, and a worker who fails to meet that need will be unlikely to be accepted in a more overtly education role. In fact, it may be necessary, particularly in the early stages of action, to restrict the community work contribution to practical support.

Whilst 'contract' may not be the most appropriate term in the current culture, nevertheless there is clearly a place for an evolving agreement with the group about what they can expect from the community worker. Ensuring, through discussion, that the worker's role is explicit may also assist the development of educational work as the activists gain knowledge and experience.

If a group, following exploration of the options open to them, decides to engage in direct action, then what does the worker do? If she/he has been working effectively, then the decision to take direct action will be based on a full discussion of the options and the implications. The nature and extent of the worker's support to the group may also be reviewed at this stage. Whether or not the support continues to be given is finally a matter for the worker and may depend on factors such as retaining credibility with the group, the specific role of the worker within the direct action tactics, and the possible reaction of the community worker's employer or manager. The real consideration, therefore, is not the ethical propriety of workers supporting direct action, but rather the potential of political action as a powerful motivating factor in adult education. Community workers should be discussing how to increase support to cross-locality political campaigns rather than debating endlessly the dilemmas of working in and against the state.

History teaches us that there is an irrefutable link between politics and education. Working class adult education has usually been most effective in the context of social and political movements. Campaigns have many of the characteristics of such movements, and when they focus on major issues such as the poll tax, VAT on fuel or water privatisation, they have the capacity to create alliances across geographical boundaries, challenging the narrow localism which actually limits educational development.

Theoretical arguments about community workers and direct action would be much more interesting and fruitful if they were based on real experience, so let's accumulate some!

Chapter 5: The Struggles of Public Sector Tenants in a Scottish Context – turning Obstacles into Opportunities

Mick Doyle, Jenny Smith, Isobel Wilson, Douglas Erdman, Sharon Donohoe, and Ann Cummings

Synopsis

In documenting the changing context of public housing in Scotland, the authors highlight the continuing need to consider the right to decent, affordable and appropriate forms of housing as a key feature of work within communities. They challenge the ability of the private sector to meet housing need, and go on to develop an analysis of the opportunities, in a complex policy environment, for tenants to develop and sustain an inclusive vision of public housing policy which can mobilise popular and political support.

Reasserting the need for social housing, they argue that tenants' organisations also have to adapt to changing situations and to engage creatively with the paradoxical nature of the debate about housing. The aspiration of 'Choice' should be made to live up to its promise: *real* freedom of choice can provide a focus for collective action which exposes the narrow interests of the market.

Strategic and practical community work support for tenants' organisations, offers possibilities for turning obstacles into opportunities for learning and action.

Introduction

It is clear that the present government doesn't like council housing: policy development over the last fifteen years has not been motivated by a desire to champion the interests of those who choose or require to rent their homes from within the public sector. Tenants have had to deal with wave upon wave of complex legislation and policy changes designed to ensure the privatisation of public sector housing and reduce the role of the local authority. It is little wonder, then, that they find it difficult to sustain the arguments and campaigns which promote their interests. Against this background Community Workers have had to re-examine practice and, in some cases, have stepped back from housing work with the view that it is 'too difficult', 'too complicated' or simply too 'old-fashioned'. It is the authors' contention that the right to decent, affordable and appropriate forms of housing are at the core of any community's aspirations and, therefore, should feature in any community work strategies to support them.

This chapter will examine recent developments in public sector housing policy in Scotland, particularly the implications of the Housing (Scotland) Act 1988 with its emphasis on tenure change, and the resultant challenges for the tenants' movement. It will further address the changing context for community work practice and suggest a strategy for future practice with the aim of generating debate amongst all those concerned.

From Beveridge to ballots

It should be obvious to all but the most casual observer that current shifts in housing policy are part of a much broader shift to the Right in social policy accentuated by the impact of Thatcherism. This shift has been characterised by a move away from the post-war consensus around a system of social welfare provision for those in need. The history of housing policy, therefore, needs to be understood in broader terms when considering the current situation. In particular the role of the Beveridge Plan, inter and post-war legislation and the political will of the post-war Labour government must be recognised as largely determining the shape, for good or ill, of what we currently know as council housing. This analysis does not attempt to argue that the current crisis in housing provision was totally precipitated by Thatcher's election in 1979, but it does recognise the fundamental role played by that government in redefining the purpose of the 'state' and its relationship with its citizens, particularly those in greatest need. Perhaps, most significantly, pre-1979 beliefs about 'rights' to a decent home have been largely replaced by an emphasis on the citizens 'responsibility' to house themselves.

The key questions for both the tenants' movement and the workers who support it, mainly revolve around the future of public sector housing. However if the tenants' movement is to be able to survive its current level of fragmentation then it must also build coalitions with others who remain as tenants but who have transferred, along with their homes, into the private or independent sectors. Irrespective of tenure, tenants must focus on building the willingness and capacity of their movement to defend and improve their conditions around a core agenda of rents, subsidy, participation and other grass roots issues such as repairs, modernisation and allocation policies. Tenants have faced an avalanche of legislation which has fundamentally affected the shape of housing for rent in the last fifteen years or so – most notably the Housing (Scotland) Act 1988 which introduced assured tenancies, tenants choice and created the national housing agency, Scottish Homes. This process started with the introduction of policies like the 'Right to Buy' and continued with massive reductions in Council subsidy with resultant effects on investment and rents. Other effects include a huge increase in the pressures on public sector tenants either to buy their homes, with the consequent and real risk of repossession, or to transfer out of the public sector in return for modernisation and at the cost of their secure tenancy rights.

The last eight years or so have seen an increase in the overall number of actual stock transfers as well as in the number of houses involved. Scottish Homes has continued to play a 'vanguard' role by promoting rapid large-scale transfers of their own stock. They have also tempted Councils who have been both starved of resources and seduced by 'new realism' to effect-large scale transfers of their stock under the auspices of 'Area Renewal' or other types of regeneration schemes (see Player in this volume). When coupled with the situation facing New Town tenants in terms of an accelerated wind-up policy, the developments outlined above illustrate the insidious progress of a 'New Right' agenda in housing which, paradoxically, offers a set of organisational opportunities for the various strands of the tenants' movement in the public sector.

The paradox of 'choice'

Scottish Homes, in particular, must be recognised as the overtly political mechanism it is. As well as its stated aims as a short-term landlord and enabling agency it also serves to subvert the role of elected councils as housing providers. This it achieves by attaching the ideological strings of the 'free market' via the classically misdescribed 'assured tenancy' to any resources available for investment. For many tenants it is this process which creates an insecure environment totally unsuitable for meeting the housing needs of a growing number of people. It is ironic then, but perhaps not surprising, that a government, whose stated objective was to remove housing from the ideological battleground has, in fact, achieved the opposite. Factors such as changing demography, the need for socio-economic mobility and new employment patterns have led to a recognition of the continuing requirement for socially-rented housing at a time when the explosion in the level of repossession, as well as the effects of recent and proposed changes in benefit rules, are proving particularly catastrophic.

Some public sector tenants have continued to maintain an organised resistance. The New Town Federations and their national grouping, the New Towns Council, have succeeded in reasserting their right to a public sector choice – though not without a sustained campaign. At the time of writing two out of five New Towns have been balloted, and both have voted overwhelmingly to transfer to their local Councils, despite the additional uncertainty caused by local government reorganisation. The others also seem likely to do so, according to recent opinion surveys. Scottish Homes tenants have been organising successfully at all levels culminating in the high profile and very successful 'Freedom of Choice Campaign'. This campaign, perhaps more than any other, has helped place the housing issue back on the political agenda, and has even encouraged some councils to join with tenants in actively resisting government policy. This campaign has been supported by the Scottish Tenants' Organisation and the Joint Tenants' Forum. The recent developments contained within the Scottish Office Consultation document 'Devolution of Power to Local Authorities' regarding giving Scottish Homes' Tenants the transfer option to local authorities, is an indication that campaign tactics are producing results. It is within these organisations that Council, New Town and Scottish Homes tenants have united around a common set of demands for the defence and improvement of the public sector. However, it must be said that whilst these campaigns have made significant gains, the fundamental issues remain. The next section of this chapter attempts to analyse some of the challenges which face the tenants' movement in Scotland at this time.

Towards a tenants' strategy

Seeking common ground

Any analysis of the way forward must begin with a period of reflection. The movement needs to critically examine itself before it can move forward towards the millennium with strategies which are both credible and effective. Such an approach must also develop an organisational framework to see that programme through. There is a need, as already stated, to develop unity across tenures where necessary. Such links need to help tenants develop policies which are both tenure and non-tenure specific. In this way independent sector tenants should be encouraged to recognise the right to a public sector choice and equality of subsidy for all tenants, whilst public sector tenants could support the independent sector in reforming the Assured Tenancy. Perhaps campaigns for ' fair tenancies for all' or 'affordable rents and a fair say for all' stand a better chance of building unity and challenging Government policy than some of the more insular, though necessary, tenure-specific campaigns of the past.

Inclusive communities

Government policy has polarised provision to such an extent that it is the most vulnerable in society who now depend most on rented housing. It is important that the tenants' movement embraces a belief in caring, supportive communities which look after the marginalised in society as well as their more mainstream members (see Arshad, and Shaw in this volume). These groups will include ethnic minority tenants, homeless people, lone parents, victims of domestic violence and those with physical and learning disabilities. A movement which does not embrace all sections of the community runs the risk of being divided in ways which weaken its overall position. Recent examples of this include the rise of the racist British National Party in Tower Hamlets and the hysteria provoked by the reintegration of people with disabilities from long-stay institutions into mainly working class communities. To deal with this agenda effectively will not be easy. It will involve the exploration of values, attitudes and fears which are well-established and deep-rooted in communities. Failure to address these will lead to serious practical as well as ideological difficulties. Such work can be difficult and may well require particular resources such as interpreters, specialist equipment and accessible meeting space.

Engaging with political processes
Strategy in the tenants movement must, by definition, take account of the political 'here and now' as well as have longer term political objectives. It is essential therefore that tenants recognise the need to engage with the political process at all levels. This need is explored more fully when we consider the community work role. It is also considered in the observations made below by the authors regarding specific proposals which we believe the tenants' movement requires to consider. These are intended to contribute to the thinking regarding formulation, planning and implementation of a tenant-led manifesto for Scotland and Britain as a whole, whilst also addressing the needs of the movement at a local level.

1. **Useful Research and Development**
    The process of critical evaluation described earlier in this chapter needs to be augmented by good use of new and existing research sources. Some of these needs may be met through the tenants' movement itself or by building links with academic institutions and 'think tanks'. Perhaps the movement needs to explore ways of commissioning research which explores the way forward for tenants, with the role of support agencies such as the Tenants' Information Service (TIS) and the Tenant Participation Advisory Service (TPAS) crucial in this regard. Arguments made elsewhere in this chapter regarding policy formation are clearly dependent on access to research and educational opportunities. Tenants need to continue to develop educational opportunities and materials at all levels. They must focus on key aspects of legislation and policy as well as ensuring that groups have access to a full range of skills-based training such as media, or negotiating skills. It will also be necessary to continue to develop opportunities to explore political and economic issues as they relate to housing issues.

2. **Popular and Political Alliances**
    Tenants need to consider what political orientation their movement should take. The Real Tenants Charter (1992) was an excellent basis for dialogue between tenants' representatives and their political supporters. Tenants need to consider the relative positions of previous political allies in the Labour

and Trade Union movement and whether they are still current. It is also necessary to find ways to lobby political parties to endorse a tenants' programme at all levels. The use of hustings as a method of putting politicians on the spot should be continued and developed at all elections. The Real Tenants' Charter should continue to be used as the basis for a sign-up campaign for political parties, opinion-forming institutions like churches and even cultural figures. In the final analysis, much of the current programme of the tenants' movement is not supported by any of the mainstream parties, and the use of tenants' candidates to highlight the issue should not be ruled out. Clearly, no analysis of the current political climate can ignore the possible advent of a Scottish Parliament. At the time of writing it seems likely that a Parliament will exist fairly soon after the next election. What is still at issue is what form it will take. Clearly this presents tenants with new opportunities for contact with a more relevant, and hopefully more receptive, political forum based on a system of proportional representation and proportionality. In the meantime the campaign for a Parliament may offer some opportunities for tenants to argue their case directly.

3.   **Organisation**
It should go without saying that there will be no progress without organisation. The key elements of this work remain constant. Tenants need to address the main issues of representation, communication and networking at local, federated and national levels. The tricky balance of building a movement which is active at all three of these levels, whilst balancing the agendas (and the energy!) between them, needs to be maintained. The movement can only remain buoyant if it is able to consolidate its grass roots support and yet generalise from specific experience to create a coherent body of national policy.

In order to make any of the developments described above concrete, tenants need not only to consider their own organisations but also the structures which support them. The policy environment tenants inhabit is more sophisticated now than it has ever been. Until now the movement has been assisted by a series of specialist resources such as the Tenants Information Service, the Tenant Participation Advisory Service and Shelter. It has also been backed up by local community work support provided by a range of agencies. The upheaval of local government reorganisation and cuts in public spending make it more important than ever for tenants to recognise their support requirements and fight to defend and improve them. Such arguments must become a coherent strand of the movements' policy agenda if other gains are to be made and underpinned. What follows is a more detailed analysis of the community work tasks required to support this overall strategy.

Community work support – implications for practice

As we have highlighted, this chapter is mainly concerned with the struggle to defend and improve public sector housing – a system of housing provision which is based on need, is publicly accountable and democratically controlled. The support for this comes from the tenants' movement itself. It comes from tenants who are campaigning in run-down estates for investment, improvements to their housing standards and homes for their children. It comes from both Scottish Homes and New Town Tenants who do not wish to transfer out of the public sector and, at a national level, through the work of The Joint Tenants' Forum and the Scottish Tenants' Organisation in promoting 'The Real Tenants' Charter'. It is important, however, to distinguish between this vision of social housing and the paternalistic, bureaucratic, unresponsive structure, which has too often been the experience of public sector tenants. Ultimately, tenants are defending the principle of accountable, effective, and fair housing services as a right. Generally, they believe these are best provided through public sector provision.

In recent years housing has been regarded by some community workers as a less important issue on the community work agenda. Some believe that the opportunities available for communities to organise around housing issues have diminished. They would argue that the new relationship between Central Government and the local state, the serious resource constraints on local authorities, and the development of formalised participation structures have all undermined the ability of community workers to assist groups to organise effectively around a housing focus. Other workers have responded to a broader community work agenda and have developed work around race issues, those affecting users of health and social services, economic development or local resource management.

Such work is clearly legitimate and, indeed, has perhaps been neglected for too long. However, a balance of issues ought to prevail and it is the pace and relative priority of these issues which will be determined by local circumstances. In this context it is the authors' experience that housing remains close to the top of the local agenda in almost every case.

Earlier in this chapter the difficulties for tenants trying to organise and promote their interests within public sector housing were illustrated. How then do community workers support tenants within this current context? The imaginative worker makes links between the various issues on the community work agenda (see Cooke in this volume), and it is this approach which allows us to recognise that black people, women, service users of community care and poor communities in general have much in common in terms of their housing needs. It is for these reasons, then, that it is necessary for community workers to re-focus their activity in order to examine housing needs, and the organisational and analytical problems they highlight. We would assert that they are as important now as they have ever been. What follows are some suggestions for practice:

The primary task
In our view, the primary task of community work remains to assist organisations at the grass roots level campaign for better conditions. This process begins with the experience of people in struggle, whether over housing or any other issue. In the housing context this demands a great deal of ground work to assist in the development of strong autonomous tenants' groups which are representative, accountable to and in touch with their communities. Only when this work is consolidated will groups be able to sustain representation at a federated or national level and, in turn, will national organisations represent the views of tenants.

Providing counter information
We can assist tenants in challenging the rhetoric of the dominant ideology which promotes values and beliefs that are consistent with it i.e. 'private, good – public, bad'. Such ideology denigrates the ideas which might challenge it. By exposing the fact that elements of Tory housing policy have failed – e.g. the private rented sector has not been substantially revitalised – we can illuminate the debate for tenants by providing counter information, giving them the confidence to promote

their own views about public sector housing. Community workers can assist this process by offering factual information and analysis of policy documents as well as supporting groups to develop effective strategies and tactics including negotiation and direct action.

Promoting collective action

Government policy has sought to individualise issues, reaching its ultimate expression in Thatcher's assertion that: 'There is no such thing as society'. The real deception here is that the traditionally powerful and privileged in society are already effectively networked through well-established structures based on class and economic power. The thrust towards individualisation, and isolation, has been aimed at the less powerful and promoted through a combination of economic blackmail and an appeal to individual greed e.g. the right to buy; shareholding in public utilities, and attacks on Trade Unions and collective bargaining on pay and conditions.

Redressing the imbalance of ownership in society requires the aggregation of individual social injustices into collective social and political action and community work has traditionally assisted beleaguered communities to do this. The need for collectivisation of issues and collective action by communities on these issues is stronger than ever in light of the above attacks. The power held by Government makes the task more difficult as do commonly-accepted perceptions that communities are more fragmented today than they were in the past. The community worker's role must, therefore, be to assist local communities to recognise, analyse and counter the factors which inhibit the taking of collective action.

Additionally, there also exists a number of factors of common concern such as – security of tenure, quality of houses, and affordable rents. Such shared concerns underpin the collective nature of tenant activity. What will change over time and across neighbourhoods is how these factors manifest themselves within communities. As community workers, we continually need to develop our own understanding, and those of the communities we work with, in order to locate the most effective avenues for collective ;action. In our view public provision is more likely to deliver a fairer distribution of power and resources than the free flow of 'market forces'.

Until recently, in the community work context, housing work has almost wholly been focused on either local authority or Scottish Homes tenants. However, as housing provision has diversified, so too have the needs of the tenants' movement. Community workers are now involved with groups who have particular needs, tenants in the private sector and homeless people. All of these present new challenges and opportunities for tenant organisation.

Responding to tenure diversification
A further illustration of the new environment relates to work with steering groups of housing associations. Some of this is controversial and community workers may have to work with tenants to make difficult decisions, particularly where investment is offered to tenants as an incentive for tenure change. Community workers may find themselves faced with a range of possible dilemmas as some tenants' groups make the transition to being landlords. We have to be clear about our role with these new emerging landlords and continuously analyse whether or not it is appropriate to continue our engagement with them. This analysis will depend on individual circumstances and relationships between workers and the group. If, as is likely, the housing association sector becomes even more 'marketised', this will have consequences for tenants. The fact that these experiences will be shared should offer new opportunities for collective action. We need to re-assert our primary role in assisting in the development of independent self-organised tenants' groups who are not compromised by trying to fulfil the landlord's functions at the same time.

Networking amongst community workers
As the authors of this chapter are part of an informal network of community workers active on housing issues throughout Scotland (established in 1987), we could not write this without making reference to the value of making alliances with other like-minded workers wherever they are to be found. Networking assists us share information, learn from each other regarding strategies and tactics for tenants' campaigns and, importantly, offer support to each other in a difficult political climate. The practical difficulties in networking should not be underestimated i.e. finding time, finding resources, co-ordinating activities. However there are clear benefits. At a time when we are under pressure from many directions, we can keep up to date about housing policy, exchange new ideas with each other, and gain an overview of the housing situation nationally.

National organisation building

The need for a strong national tenants' movement has never been more evident with attacks on public sector housing, Scottish Homes' intention of relinquishing its landlord role and the 'wind up' of the New Towns. This has resulted in a growth of local groups and federations, and a strengthening of national organisations. Community workers at a neighbourhood level should assist groups form federations, and eventually join national organisations. Where at all practicable, workers should also offer assistance and support directly to the national organisations, particularly where such work may secure resources for those organisations themselves.

The whole question of support to the tenants' movement has been a vexed one over the years. A major step forward would be to recognise that tenants now face an increasingly sophisticated policy environment. Such an environment could be enriched by a recognition that the tenants' movement requires a range of specialist support. The Tenants' Information Service, Tenants' Participation Advisory Service, Housing Association Chartered Accountancy Service and the Legal Service Agency fit this description, although their service is often not free at the point of need.

When the requirement for community work support, whether from the statutory or voluntary sectors, is considered, it may be helpful, given the current resource situation, if tenants bid for such support as part of an integrated campaign. Such resources are essential to develop and underpin the work of the tenants' movement itself. In this regard, the effects of local government reorganisation must be taken into account. A number of tenants' federations have, in recent years, employed their own staff, funded from a variety of sources – including rent levies. This can only be of benefit to the movement. The long-term funding for a national tenants' organisation remains unresolved and this will continue to contribute to its weakness.

The Joint Tenants' Forum and the Scottish Tenants' Organisation have produced their own policy statement 'The Real Tenants Charter' which raise the following demands:

• Investment – a costed national assessment of need
• A New Housing Act – financial measures to meet identified need
• Case for subsidy – stating grounds for subsidising public sector
• Tenure – repeal of Housing (Scotland) Act 1988

*   Tenant participation – need for statutory measures to ensure tenant participation
*   Homelessness – 'Code of Guidance' to be made statutory

Community workers should be using this as a framework for raising housing issues and in assisting tenants formulate demands. The Scottish New Town tenants' success in gaining District Councils as a transfer option should not be underestimated and, indeed, offers encouragement to the Scottish Homes tenants who are currently denied this choice.

Building new alliances
Radical Community work principles of the 1970s and 1980s identified the need for tenants to work with the Trade Union and Labour movement with a view to linking community and workplace struggles (see Cooke in this volume). For those who attempted this, success was very limited and tenants' groups were often viewed at Trades Councils meetings, for example, as an irritant and outwith the 'real issues'. This suspicion led to inevitable disillusionment with the potential for such joint action. Although we would still advocate this approach, caution is advised as to its effectiveness. Care should be taken not to make assumptions regarding the interests of the various partners in joint work of this kind. The labour movement is now, of course, quite a different force after fifteen years of anti-Trade Union legislation, and tenant' groups have to assess the benefits of making such alliances in the current context. It is to its credit that the tenants' movement continues to challenge when more substantial organisations have bent to the weight of 'the new right' project. The Labour Party – or 'New Labour' as it is now known – has publicly declared its hostility to public ownership and traditional socialist ideals. As it has wooed what it sees as the more important middle class vote many of the economically active working class have taken up the 'Right to Buy', leaving the remaining tenants isolated and feeling like second class citizens.

Without leadership and class solidarity, tenuous as it has been, many tenants now feel marginalised and excluded. There are some recent examples, however, of success in forming alliances e.g. 'The Freedom of Choice Campaign', in which the Scottish Homes' Tenants have won the support of Scottish Labour M.P.s and local authorities. This approach also applies to the work of the Scottish New Town Tenants, who formed the Scottish Local Authorities and New Towns

Campaign (S.L.A.A.N.T.). We would also argue that there is a need for tenants to look for other allies such as the media, the churches, cultural and environmental organisations, pop stars, the women's movement and other single-issue campaigns. Perhaps community workers could also encourage tenants to look for alliances in the European context, for example through the European Poverty Programmes. Scottish Homes tenants' groups are currently considering the possibility of using the European Court of Justice to raise issues of denial of rights. Other tenants' groups have used a European route to access funds for housing improvements. Indeed, in the future it may be worth exploring links with other elements of the embryonic European tenants' movement.

Another key arena which should be addressed by tenants is the Scottish constitutional context. All of the opposition parties support some measure of devolution and it seems quite likely, therefore, that the tenants' movement will need to build a response. In terms of short term pragmatic objectives, direct representation could perhaps be sought in the recently-formed Scottish 'Senate'. Such a strategy would allow tenants to maximise publicity opportunities whilst acting as part of a broad-based coalition for constitutional change, giving the national movement an opportunity to determine its position on constitutional issues.

Conclusion

So what conclusions can we draw from all of this? On the one hand state support for rented housing in the public sector has been dramatically reduced. In real terms there has been a cut in subsidy of £91m since 1983. Tenure has altered radically with a 20% increase in owner occupation since 1979 and a corresponding reduction in public sector renting of 14% over the same period. On the other hand, the government has not always found it easy to fully implement its policy agenda. The formulation of policy is not an exact science; indeed the very existence of government policy initiatives has tended to highlight loopholes around which communities can organise, turning obstacles into opportunities. It is certainly true, for example, that whilst bankers and financial institutions are motivated primarily by profit, they have been reluctant to embrace the 'pick a landlord' or 'rent to mortgage' schemes. It seems that the private sector have not responded to the market opportunities created by Tory housing policy precisely because they recognise the risks associated with reconciling the needs of the rented housing 'market' with the needs of tenants. The fact that only 9% of rented housing in Scotland is in the private or Housing Association sectors seems to confirm this. Since, ultimately, the private sector will only be motivated by the potential for a return on their investment it may be that, in the final analysis, the policies will fail for these reasons

It is unfortunate, then, that there seems to be little political will amongst the dominant opposition parties to exploit this situation. What is clear is that the tenants' movement will have to depend on its own resources in order to achieve change. These resources should be considerable as, at the time of writing, there are 700,000 properties still in the public sector. The challenge, then, is to assist tenants organise to secure provision based on need.

The ideological thrust of 'marketisation' and the transfer of responsibility from the state to the individual are clearly unpopular amongst tenants. In this context the lessons of the Poll Tax Campaign suggest that angry people take action (see Rosendale in this volume). The residualisation of council housing, increased homelessness, decreasing investment, and the possibility of foreclosures by banks on independent sector landlords are all factors which suggest that people will continue to seek community work support in arguing for a return to effectively funded state provision.

The fact that tenants face these challenges demands that the tenants' movement continues to seek alliances wherever opportunities exist and continue to protect and develop the resources which will allow it to flourish. Above all else, tenants must resist the pressure to take more and more responsibility for managing the tensions between needs and resources and maintain their crucial role in representing the tenants' side in the landlord/tenant relationship.

These factors clarify the need to protect the concept of truly independent advice, information and assistance to tenants on housing issues. This objective in itself will be difficult to deliver in the context of local government reorganisation and continued restrictions in public expenditure. Publicly defending our corner has always been anathema to community workers – perhaps we can no longer afford this luxury.

In addition to working with tenants on the 'product' issues of housing we need to re-affirm our educational goals in 'process' terms. Indeed, these objectives remain central to the role of community workers in assisting tenants to understand, operate within and, where necessary, challenge their political environment. These elements of the task remain central despite the fact that they are poorly understood and undervalued by our funders. Opportunities created by decentralised approaches to housing management, tenure change and tenant involvement in housing management plans ensure there are still opportunities for community workers. The continuing role in more established issues like rents, repairs or allocations simply serve to underpin this fact. What is new is the nature of the coalitions which require to be built across tenures and with other groups concerned with health, poverty and other issues with a housing dimension.

Radical community work practice must continue to support and defend the rights of disadvantaged communities to self-organise and campaign around issues of importance to them. In our view there are few issues more important to people in working class communities than the provision of a decent roof over their heads. It is to be hoped that those who currently determine the shape of our social policy are about to learn that there are also few issues more motivating.

Acknowledgements

This chapter reflects the views of the authors in their personal capacity. Thanks to Yvonne Fitzgerald for her patience and typing skills; Alan Ferguson, Jim Lister and Samantha Reeves for their help and advice.

Bibliography

Barrhead Community Council (1984). *Housing Heroes – The Struggles of a Small Town. 1919–1939*

Bryant and Bryant (1982). *Change and Conflict.* University Press, Aberdeen, 1982

Craig, Derricourt and Loney (1982). *Community Work and the State.* RKP

CDP (1986) *Whatever Happened to Council Housing?* CDP Intelligence Unit

Jacob S, (1977). *The Right to a Decent Home.* RKP

Jacobs S and Popple K, (1995). *Community Work in the 1990s.* Spokesman

London–Edinburgh Weekend Return Group (1979). *In and Against the State.* Pluto Press

Midwinter, Keating and Mitchell (1991) Eds. *Politics and Public Policy in Scotland.* Macmillan

Robertson D, (1992). *Choices for Tenants – An examination of issues arising from the Housing (Scotland) Act 1988.* SCVO

Smith M, (1984). *A Guide to Housing,* 3rd Edition, Housing Centre Trust

Socialists Housing Activists' Workshop, (1980). *Socialism and Housing Action – Workshop Papers*

Ward C, (1979). *When Shall We Build Again.* Pluto Press

The Real Tenants' Charter, available from Scottish Tenants' Organisation, 25 St. Andrews Street, Glasgow.

Chapter 6: Out of the Quagmire: Community Care – Problems and Possibilities for Radical Practice

Mae Shaw

Synopsis

The quagmire of community care is the focus of this chapter. The author exposes some of the contradictions, conflicts and convergences which reflect the different interests involved in current policy development. Within the wider context of the restructuring of welfare, it is argued that 'care' has become a site of struggle in which narrow sectional interests are posed against fundamental ideas of what constitutes a 'caring' society.

Recognising the voices of new social movements coalescing around issues of welfare, the author argues that the insights they offer provide a critique of welfare which goes beyond sterile dichotomies: reconnecting the collective with the specific, the political with the personal. The metaphor of dependency offers no real possibilities for agency. A new discourse of care must be constructed in which dependence and burden are not the necessary outcomes.

Such a discourse requires a more finely nuanced understanding of identity and structure, linking common material position with differential experience. In this way solidarity in difference can be fostered. A tentative framework is offered which recognises the potential of community work to engage creatively with the tensions and contradictions generated in the quagmire of community care.

Introduction

'Caring should be the place we begin, and not end our analysis of modern society' (Graham, 1986)

Recent developments in community care, in particular the 1989 legislation, have had significant implications for all aspects of community work practice: from a formalised role in 'delivering' user-involvement in the provision of care to the sometimes unanticipated and often disruptive presence of de-hospitalised individuals within existing community groups. The community work response, however, has been partial and largely reactive. This response has taken four broad forms. First, a knee-jerk reaction: if the Tories say it's good, it must be bad. This is related to the second response: State/public is good, individual/private is bad. Third, 'care' is a social work issue – nothing to do with community work. Fourth, the policy imperatives of 'Care in the Community' rely on a community work response; therefore, we must respond.

There is, however, a fifth position which is gathering interest – a position which recognises the opportunities presented by community care to connect with radical community work practice. It is this radical potential that is the focus of this chapter.

In order to develop a framework for engaging purposefully with community care, it is necessary to start, not from pragmatism, but from analysis of wider issues to do with the relationship between people, the state and welfare. The starting point for such an assessment of the opportunities for purposeful practice must be a recognition of the intrinsic contradictions of social policy, the different – and often competing – interests at play, and the potential gap between intention and outcome. The relationship between community work and policy is not straightforward. Indeed, historically, a key tenet of radical practice has been the need to use rather than obscure these inherent contradictions to develop a practice which doesn't simply 'deliver community' at every turn of policy regardless of purpose and context. The distinction, therefore, between the functions of policy (both implicit and explicit) and the purposes of radical community work practice is a key one in locating the problems and possibilities for critical engagement with the current policy context.

This context includes the extensive privatisation of former publicly accountable and provided services. In fact the marketisation of care can be seen as an exemplar of the way in which the dual economic and ideological imperatives of rolling back the state and the creation of internal markets are being pursued. In this process responsibility is shifted from the state to the individual, family or community. Whilst this characterisation of the New Right position is necessarily somewhat over-simplified, it can nevertheless be argued that a crucial function of community care is precisely to provide the necessary framework for this transfer of responsibility from the public to the private domains.

It is the notion of privatised obligation, with its implications of dependency, which is being challenged by those new social groupings which have coalesced around issues arising from the New Right's restructuring of welfare – organisations of disabled people for example, such as People First and the Coalition of Disabled People and those which have developed to represent the interests of carers. These previously-discounted voices act as a critique of welfare and seek to re-assert a social obligation which recognises equal rights and social justice as its moral driving force. The insights offered by these emergent social movements provide a critique of welfare which goes beyond the sterile dichotomy of state versus individual, thus reconnecting the democratic and egalitarian project of progressive community work with the concrete realities of people in communities.

The distinction between private and social obligation also makes it possible to contrast care as a privatised solution with care as an aspect of collective human responsibility which embodies a vision for society as a whole. Invoking a society in which social harmony is the outcome of democratic and egalitarian relations, Milliband (1994) argues for the cultivation of a 'socialised individualism' which recognises that concern and provision for the best material conditions of all members of society is in the interests of *all* its members. This is in sharp contrast to the 'authoritarian collectivism' which, it is argued, characterised much social welfare provision in the past, and negative experience of which made it so vulnerable to attack by the New Right. It also challenges the possessive individualism implicit in the notions of care as either commodity or personal obligation. It is the argument of this paper that community care offers community workers an opportunity to play a significant part in cultivating precisely that combination of collective responsibility and individual aspiration which is implicit in Milliband's notion of 'socialised individualism'.

The Context and the Contest

The context in which the community care legislation developed was a changing and contradictory one, with both national and international dimensions. As Mayo (1994) argues, changes in the global economy caused increasing polarisation between and within both nations and regions. The economic miracle, with its promise of a 'trickle-down effect' which would improve peoples' lives, failed to materialise. As a consequence, whilst social needs increased, the economic capacity and political will to meet them were progressively reduced, leaving those most disadvantaged in the process to fend for themselves. Community care legislation, therefore, has to be located in the wider context of the 'crisis of welfare' which emerges from the cynical link between welfare and affordability.

This changing context of welfare, then, became a focus for the politics of priority. In this sense, current developments in the long history of community care reflect a more general and fundamental crisis, recognised by all political interests and positions – albeit from very different perspectives and with very different prescriptions. This convergence of interest has led many to think of 'care' as a key site of struggle in which narrow sectional interests are posed against fundamental ideas of what constitutes a 'good and caring' society. There is clear evidence that, despite general election results which would seem to indicate the contrary, there is widespread public support for a significant degree of collectivism. Furthermore, it should be emphasised that Scotland has consistently rejected the individualising hegemony of the New Right.

Jeffries (1994) argues that there is a link between 'vision' and 'power'. It is in making this link that the new social movements have been particularly significant. These movements, which have coalesced around or out of their concrete experiences of welfare have, by challenging problem definitions and refusing to accept individualising explanations and labels, begun to develop a vision of a genuinely enabling society. This brings into sharp focus an alternative and potentially radical notion of 'community' which can be seen as the distinctive territory of these movements. By recognising 'care' as a site of struggle, we can begin to frame a practice which starts from the ambivalence of 'community', highlighting its contradictions and searching for opportunities.

It has been argued that the integrative function of the dominant paradigm in community work paradoxically offers potential for autonomous movements and organisations to identify spaces in which to operate (see Cockburn, 1977). By underpinning 'community' through policy and by provision of resources – not least the employment of community workers – the State creates a contradictory situation in which participation, for example, becomes a 'two-edged sword'. The commitment to user-involvement in the community care legislation has been identified by many as a key 'space' for previously excluded voices to be heard as citizens, not simply as consumers (see Croft and Beresford, 1992).

'Community', therefore, can be deployed for both progressive and reactionary purposes. For example, the spurious 'unity' of the communitarian vision has been used by parties across the political spectrum for both instrumental and ideological purposes to combine the restructuring of welfare within a free market economy with the construction of an idealised and deeply conservative subsidiarity. 'Community' as neighbourhood offers particular utility in this respect, where 'the community' becomes the arbiter of rights and responsibilities, and 'solutions' are readily available at local level. In contrast, the iconoclastic adherence to difference and diversity, which is characteristic of post-modern positions, challenges the assumption of inclusive community. It is certainly clear to anyone who has worked in a local setting, for example, that 'community' can be as much about exclusion and closure as inclusion and solidarity. In fact, it could be argued that its ideological value within market-led politics relies on those very notions of homogeneity and harmonious relations which create the boundaries that define exclusion – who's in and who's out. Inclusive practice has to be painstakingly constructed, not unproblematically assumed as a 'technical additive'. The focus then becomes the *exclusive community*, not those who are excluded from access to it.

The concept of the exclusive community shifts attention usefully to the distinction between 'the community' and 'communities' as a way of connecting the collective with the specific, rather than constituting different and incompatible aspirations. As Martin (1992) argues, community workers find themselves ' ... working towards "community" by working with"communities"'. This demands an engagement with the broader community, taking opportunities to extend the notion of who is 'bonafide' and, in the context of community care, ensuring that we don't simply reinforce the 'hospitalisation' of the community in place of the institution (Tudor 1990/91). The recognition of structured and structural inequalities as barriers to the inclusive community needs also to be addressed as the context in which individual behaviour and prejudices develop. Power relations need to be made explicit; power which is invisible cannot be addressed.

The flexible currency of 'community' and the power to define it can therefore be seen as a key arena in the struggle over community care. This helps to explain the broad support which met publication of the Griffiths Report (HMSO, 1988), forerunner to the community care legislation. However, if the notion of 'community' can be seen as both persuasive and elastic in this context, then the added imperative which 'care' implies offered perhaps the sharpest focus for cross-political attention, including the expression of previously discounted voices, which fundamentally challenged the parameters of the discourse.

Changing the climate or changing the weather?

This section attempts to present the key convergences and differences in the debate over care. This necessarily involves summarising complex positions and is intended primarily to illuminate the broad terrain of policy development.

The contest over 'care' has had professional, political, philosophical and popular dimensions with partial convergence on particular aspects. Despite fundamental conflicts between the free-market ideas of the New Right, reflected in government policy, and the concept of universal provision, as embodied in the reformist left, for example, there does seem to be broad concensus on the need for change in definitions of 'care', but for very different reasons. For the right, it is clear that community care represents sound common sense. In a population where the dependency ratio is becoming unsustainable, community care becomes a cheap alternative. It also fulfils ideological functions – strengthening the institution of the family, reinforcing the traditional role of women, and the cohesion of the community. However, in the context of the 1980s, it was also seen by many as a counter to what was becoming an issue of concern regarding the inappropriate organisation, in both financial and human terms, of the care of those who depended on it.

Theoretical developments such as Goffman's (1968) studies of the dehumanising effects of institutionalisation and Wolfensberger's (1974) concern with 'normalization' had already influenced the thinking of many welfare professionals. At the same time drug developments had made maintenance of 'reasonable' life outside of institutions a possibility. Revelations about abuses in long-stay mental institutions, together with exposure of the effects of incarceration on the morbidity of old people, also fed a growing sense of public unease.

In this sense, community care resonated with widespread popular and professional concern in a way which reinforced the New Right project, albeit unintentionally. Thatcherite intervention effectively exploited this context to maximise support.

At a broader political and philosophical level, however, it could be argued that community care also exposes a more abstract but nonetheless significant contest between modernist ideas, which emphasise large-scale, structural ways of making sense of the world, and the ideas of post-modernism which focus on the diversity and fragmentary nature of 'lived experience' to challenge the homogeneity and standardisation implicit in the modernist account which, it is argued, characterised the organisation of the old-style Welfare State. So, whilst the context of care provided a traditional battleground on which left and right argued superiority of vision, it also offered a focus for the struggle between 'old' left orthodoxy and the 'new' left. The latter sought to distance itself from what it saw as the bureaucratic, paternalistic and wasteful machinery of the welfare state. This had the effect of highlighting the emergence of new social movements with their emphasis on differentiation and 'voice', questioning many of the assumptions surrounding 'care', and demanding the right to define the problem for themselves.

Convergence and Difference

The issue which created the most intense interest was the redefinition of the relationship between the 'cared for' and those providing the care. For the new right ideologues the dependent 'client' was anathema. In the process of the privatisation of 'care', the 'welfare client' would become the customer or, in the language of service rather than product, the 'consumer' or 'user'. For those articulating 'the consumer' perspective with the emphasis as much on identity and the right to participate as on material improvements, the professional/client relationship represented a necessarily dependent one. Oliver (1990) argues that independence means different things depending on which end of that relationship you are! The professional view, often dominated by the gate-keeping of resources, is that independence means 'doing things without help' or 'alone'. For disabled people, on the other hand, independence means the ability to be in control of decisions about one's life – a 'state of mind ... not contingent on a healthy body'.

This distinction allows us to engage with the politics of practice in a way which begins to take us out of the quagmire of community care. Exposing the seeming convergence and identifying the relationship between interests and purposes makes it possible to see how real popular concerns have been used to legitimate the dilution of collective responsibility. The insights which emerge from this analysis offer us an opportunity to reconnect the democratic aspirations of new social movements with those enduring egalitarian principles which demand a collective response.

The State Provides?

As highlighted earlier, the emphasis in modernist accounts of welfare is on state-provided, universal services 'from the cradle to the grave', a conception at the heart of the post-war settlement of which the Welfare State was the key component. However, the most trenchant criticisms of this position revolve around precisely this interpretation of universality. Whilst concerns range from those to do with implementation and substance to more fundamental issues of principle – some want to change the climate of care, others the weather – the idea which dominates, is 'participation' whether as 'customer', as some would have it, or 'democratic citizen', as the new social movements would have it. The assertion that a democratic deficit existed in relation to welfare provision was central to the critiques which emerged in relation to community care.

The substantive argument focused on the universal *delivery* of 'care' as distinct from its availability, challenging the ability of the state to recognise, never mind meet, differential needs. This inability, it was argued, led to the dehumanising effects of 'the mass production of welfare', which created dependence, regarding people as objects rather than subjects (where they were regarded as subjects, it was as 'social problems') (see Mann, 1986). This essentially paternalistic 'we know best' approach did not connect with the concrete realities of those implicated in the process, thus effectively denying them voice. The concentration on the ends neglected the means. Together then, these features of 'old-style welfarism' created not only dependence, but also divisions between carers and cared-for obscuring both the complexity of caring relationships and potential common interests.

The traditional left, defenders of both the Welfare State (particularly since it was being dismantled root and branch) and democratic voice therefore found itself in a contradictory position regarding community care which effectively marginalised interests which should have been central. This was compounded by the threat of a new kind of popular resistance, which did not seem to connect with traditional politics. The vacuum created by trying to sustain this untenable position was filled by a range of interests. These included some traditional combatants around issues of welfare, particularly feminists, but also a growing number of new groupings which saw the space created by the debate about 'care' as an opportunity to raise crucial issues of exclusion and discrimination.

Out of the quagmire – insights and experience

Feminist critiques of welfare emphasise the contradictions of state provision and, in particular, focus on the patriarchal nature of the Welfare State and its role in reproducing the sexist structures of wider society. Such critiques claim that state welfare is centrally involved in the construction of the family wage system and the woman as 'housewife', and that social welfare therefore rests on the assumption of women as essentially dependent, domestic labourers. However, since this analysis is also predicated on the notion of care as a burden, feminists find themselves in an ambivalent position in relation to community care. Having pointed out the inadequacies of the Welfare State, they are no more satisfied with an alternative which relies on women to an arguably greater extent whilst 'silently confining them to the private sphere without so much as even mentioning them' (Wilson, 1982). In rejecting community care on this basis, Dalley (1988), for example, advocates the provision of small-scale, publicly-provided collective care in localised settings as an expression of 'the wider responsibility which society as a whole has for its members'. Ironically, of course, such care would be provided largely by low-paid working class women.

Caring for and caring about
In shedding some useful theoretical light on the highly-charged notion of care, Dalley (1988) distinguishes between 'caring for' and 'caring about'. The former is to do with the tasks of 'tending' another person, whilst the latter is to do with 'feelings for' another person. However, it is the conflation of these two notions in the dominant hegemony which 'form(s) a unitary integral part of a woman's nature', whereby it is all too easy to argue that if you care about somebody you will also be prepared to care for them.

Conversely, if you are not prepared to care for them, then it is clear that you do not care about them. This emotional equation has been used most effectively by the New Right both as a means of privatising the responsibility for 'caring for' and of reinforcing the hegemony so necessary to sustain women's role as prime carers. Thus 'Women have internalised the altruistic label; society has capitalised on it' (Dalley, 1988)

It has been argued that the most insidious exercise of power is to limit people's perceptions so that they conform to a dominant view to which they see no alternative, no matter how much it seems to contradict their objective interests (see Lukes, 1974). In this way, 'hegemony depends not so much on consent as resignation' (Milliband, 1994). To see such conformity as a problem for practice shifts the focus to a recognition of 'latent demand' as an equally legitimate, if less visible, 'claim' on community work support. Limited perceptions of both 'self-identity' and material expectations have been a key feature of the provision of care – for those at both ends of the caring relationship. This understanding, in educational terms, reveals the necessity of opening up the discourse about roles and experience, the embeddedness of these in social relations of power and the need to see the relevance of this discourse to the wider community, not just those 'communities of interest' most disadvantaged by its limitations.

The practical and emotional obligations placed on families, particularly women, arising from the dominant hegemony are also of particular concern for those who are defined as dependent in the process. It is for the lack of recognition of this convergence of interests that many feminists are taken to task – in particular by their disabled sisters.

Care as burden or opportunity?
The conceptual separation of the 'dependant' from 'the family' (or indeed 'the community') is at the core of the perception of care as either burden or opportunity. Walmsley (1993) argues that the formulation of caring within the family as oppression has emerged from a largely white middle-class perspective. She goes on to observe that the experience of both black and white working-class women has often been that of enforced caring *outside* the family as a means of supporting their children. From this perspective, she reasons, caring for their own family might be regarded as a way of 'resisting racial and

class oppression'. If we are asking, therefore, who is involved in caring for members of the family, it is not enough to assume that this is only determined by gender. With changing work patterns, for example, many more men fulfil the full-time caring role. Race and class are also significant. The single mother who can afford to pay a nanny (often a young working-class woman) may be less disadvantaged than low-paid parents in a nuclear family. Further, in re-evaluating care as an activity from the perspective of disabled women, Walmsley argues that for some women who are denied the opportunity to become carers, caring becomes a valued activity to be sought rather than an oppressive burden to be avoided.

In arguing that community care policies are based on an ideology of dependence – 'them and us' – Morris (1991/92) and others accuse feminist insistence on care as a burden of further reinforcing that dependency. The dissociation of 'family' from 'dependants' is extended in this account, to 'women' and 'dependants'. In an article examining the possibilities of developing non-sexist alternatives in community care, Finch (1984) asks: 'Can we envisage any version of community care which is not sexist? If we cannot then we need to say something about how we imagine such people can be cared for in ways which we find acceptable'. In a rejoinder Morris, a disabled feminist, asks who Finch means when she says 'we' and whether 'we' are included in the term 'such people'. What this debate highlights is a continuity in conventional wisdom about care which has survived various critiques, reflecting a consistent failure to identify with the interests and experiences of those who need care – the 'omissions' of policy. This failure to recognise and validate differential experience has been a key notion in the development of new social movements around welfare issues. It has also led many to the conclusion that the arena of cultural politics may hold more prospect for transformative action than that of formal politics. The logic of this analysis is that community workers should be well-placed to contribute to the process of reconnecting the cultural politics of the new social movements with underlying social and economic structures.

There are two trends within feminist thought which have broader utility here. Firstly, recognition of 'differences' (plural) acknowledges a growing understanding of the differentially-lived experience of women on the basis of class, race, sexuality, age and ability. Secondly, celebration of 'difference' (singular) assumes that all women share the same experience and needs and that there is something innate and/or essential about the category 'woman', 'black' or 'disabled'(see Meekosha, 1993). In this account, the values of nurturing and caring are presented as natural, women-only values. The logic of this kind of essentialism, of course, is that it actively excludes. If, for example, caring is seen as an important symbol of womanhood, are disabled women, who are on the whole excluded from being carers, in 'no woman's land' (Morris, 1991/92)? Secondly, there is a danger that essentialist conceptions which can emerge from discussions about difference can as easily be invoked to preserve homogeneity – the project of the New Right. The definition of women as natural carers, for example, has value for a range of competing purposes. What is more, the reification of difference experienced within particular forms of oppression can conceal commonalities: 'any attempt to discuss commonalities undermines attempts to discuss difference and vice versa' (Meekosha, 1993). The contested terrain of community care therefore offers opportunities to challenge all forms of reductionist and exclusive essentialism and to begin to forge solidarity out of difference.

The 'other'!
What has emerged most significantly from the discussion of difference and diversity is the question of 'voice'. This has considerable rhetorical force within community care legislation, and yet it also has particular salience for those who have been most severely excluded and regarded as 'other' – often defined out of society itself. Branson and Miller (1989) assert the necessity to capitalist economies of those it constructs as 'the other': 'Their existence is of central importance for their asocial presence – they are "there" reinforcing the social, cultural normality of others'. Consequently we need 'the other' to constitute the norms which are necessary to justify inequalities and to distinguish the deserving from the undeserving. The construction of 'the other' performs a hegemonic function in many marxian and feminist accounts of the world. Not only does it marginalise the objects of its attention, but it also reinforces the exclusive legitimacy of those who are included. It is now widely recognised, for example, that the representation of the 'red menace' at the height of the Cold War as 'the other' not only justified massive arms expenditure but also allowed those in the West to consider their culture as self-evidently superior. This in turn justified all efforts (persuasive or coercive) to preserve it. An historical understanding of community development,

for example, demonstrates its utility, in both colonial and domestic settings as a counter-insurgency strategy – reducing the threat of subversive factions. This process can only be understood in terms of an assumed and threatening 'other'. Indeed, it has been argued that the integrative function of community work can only be understood in terms of the discourse of 'the other'.

The construct of 'the other' can be seen to operate ideologically through individuals and communities as well as institutions. Mead (in Stuart and Thompson, 1995) argues that it is through the very process of how we see ourselves and are defined by others that we are placed in a social hierarchy :

> 'Whilst our social institutions create the material parameters within which we are able to function in society; our class position, gender, ethnicity and so on, it is through the process of forming our self identity that we unconsciously internalise the power relations of broader society'

In acknowledging the part that such ideological constructs have played historically in discrimination against marginalised groups by the organised working class, Milliband (1994) puts the blame squarely on the competitive and exploitative nature of capitalist society. Thus 'injuries of class' fester in a system in which workers have sought to improve their bargaining position by preventing access to women, black, disabled and older people. 'Discrimination is then rationalised by ideological constructs [in the form of] ... stereotypes ... [which] acquire a life of their own and become an autonomous part of the culture.' In making this argument, Milliband clearly grounds discrimination and exclusion in the social contexts in which they occur, linking issues of identity to material conditions and locating specific experiences of particular marginalised groups in the common experience of inequality and exclusion. The reconnection of structural explanations with specific experiences is crucial if issues of power are to be addressed. All too often 'difference can avoid discussions of power' (Meekosha 1993). It is these reconnections and the opportunities they generate that potentially offer an agenda for radical community work practice.

Community work and community care: an agenda for radical practice

A new paradigm of 'care' needs to be developed and articulated which seeks to resolve the contradictions of 'authoritarian collectivism' whilst incorporating its insights into the nature of social inequality and its aspirations towards a more just and egalitarian social order. Marris (1987) argues that the metaphors we use to express social relationships circumscribe the discourse – the framework within which meanings are ascribed validity. The metaphor of dependency offers no real possibilities for Human agency. The implications of this for practice are outlined in the following tentative framework which recognises the potential of community work to engage creatively with the tensions and contradictions generated by the quagmire of community care.

- **Engaging critically with people's experience:** This is the only way of developing a curriculum for social action. The key resource for transformative practice is 'lived experience'; whether this be, for example, of unemployment, full-time caring for a disabled spouse, trade unionism, or long-term institutionalisation. This means recognising the complexity of such experience and the dilemmas of choice inherent in it, never reducing our understanding to one limited (and limiting) dimension.

- **Making common cause with legitimate voices of 'resistance':** This means not substituting one professional agenda for another; recognising the rights (and expertise) of those who live with the consequences of policy-making to define the 'problem' for themselves (see Petrie in this volume). It also means supporting struggles *against* discrimination and *for* civic political and social rights.

- **Developing a more finely nuanced understanding of identity and structure:** The fundamental connection between the two should be enhancing rather than limiting. Too often the role of community work has been seen as simply challenging labelling and changing attitudes, without recognising the material and political context within which they develop, thereby individualising the problem and the solution. On the other hand the struggle to make activities purposeful and accessible to all potentially enhances the experiences and understandings for all involved.

- **Challenging 'community' as an essentially unifying idea:** It is necessary to challenge any notion of 'inclusive practice' which means nothing more than a 'technical additive' strategy, recognising 'exclusion' as the logical outcome of an unequal society (see Petrie in this volume). Focussing on the exclusive community shifts practice from an adaptive to a proactive one. The 'management of diversity' (Meekosha, 1993), which requires groups and needs to be essentially linked, can conceal commonalities. This stalemate can only be broken by reconstructing the notion of 'community' in a way which accommodates differential experience, recognising it as necessary to the development of a more inclusive reality, whilst seeking common ground with others – solidarity in difference.
- **Fostering alliances:** Issues of identity need to be linked with material position, highlighting conditions experienced in common with others, e.g. through poverty (see Cooke in this volume). Demands for sensitivity to difference and recognition of the specific experiences of highly-marginalised groups must be accommodated within an expanded meaning of solidarity if they are not to result in division, fragmentation and ultimate defeat: ' ... signification of difference has ... often led to increased levels of conflict, hostility and resentment between social groups who otherwise share a common material experience' (Miller and Bryant, 1990).
- **Solidarity in difference:** By seeking to turn personal troubles into public issues, community workers can begin to see their role as 'offering inspiration to dispossessed groups and individuals' (Hawker, 1989) by exposing, on the one hand, the structural barriers to those who have internalised the limitations imposed on them and, on the other, by sustaining groups which are transforming stigma into pride.
- **Intention and outcome:** The gap between intention and outcome offers opportunities for creative practice, but it requires both a clear sense of purpose and a strategic approach. Making the critical distinction between 'purpose' and 'function' can provide a starting point from which to 'mobilise communities for action through struggles for power, rather than the cheaper management of targeted state services' (Meekosha, 1993).

- **Critical participation**: The practice which emerges from a strategic consideration of the opportunities for increased 'voice' in community care, seeking out possibilities to address the democratic aspirations of highly-marginalised groups, is very different from that which substitutes for this a limited idea of user-involvement and 'customer care'. This key distinction between 'democratic' and 'consumer' approaches offers community workers a way to foster genuinely democratic voice, minimising the dangers of incorporation (Croft and Beresford, 1992).

- **Beyond the discourse of dependence**: The relationship between how we think, what we say and what we do is crucial:

  'The idea of finding one's voice or having a voice assumes a primacy in talk discourse, writing and action ... only as subjects can we speak. As objects, we remain voiceless – our beings defined and interpreted by others .... Awareness of the need to speak, to give voice to the varied dimensions of our lives, is one way [to begin] the process of education for critical consciousness' (hooks, quoted in Giroux, 1992).

Conclusion: Out of the quagmire

A new discourse of caring needs to be constructed – one in which dependence and burden are not the necessary outcomes. We need to be able to think in a way which does not reduce certain groups and individuals to 'the other', one-dimensional bundles of need, whilst recognising that none of us are entirely independent. It is precisely the recognition of such interdependence, at a fundamental level, that should be fought for, fostered and resourced. The quagmire of community care presents a real opportunity for community workers to be at the heart of this struggle.

Acknowledgement

Thanks to Ian Martin for his comments on several drafts of this chapter.

References

Branson, J. and Miller, D. (1989). Beyond integration policy: the deconstruction of disability. *In:* L. Barton, ed. *Integration Myth or Reality*. Falmer Press

Cockburn, C. (1977). *Local Government as Local State*. Pluto Press

Croft, S. and Beresford, P. (1992). The politics of participation. *Critical Social Policy*. Issue 35

Dalley, G. (1988). *Ideologies of Caring: Rethinking Community and Collectivism*. Basingstoke: Macmillan Education

Dominelli, L. (1990). *Women and Community Action*. Venture Press

Finch, J. (1984). Community care: developing non-sexist alternatives. *Critical Social Policy*. Issue 9

Giroux, H. (1992). *Border Crossings*. Routledge

Goffman, E (1961). *Asylums*. Pelican

Graham, H. (1994) *In:* V. George and P. Wilding. *Welfare and Ideology*. Harvester Wheatsheaf

Hawker, M. (1989). Consumer participation as community development: action in an ambiguous context. *Community Development Journal*. 24(4)

HMSO (1988). Griffiths Report: *Community Care: An Agenda for Action*

Jeffries, H. (1994). Community organising in the United States: coalescing a diversity of discourses. *In:* S. Jacobs and K. Popple, eds. *Community Work in the 1990s*. Spokesman

Lukes, S. (1974). *Power: A Radical View*. London: Macmillan

Mann, K. (1986). The making of a claiming class: the neglect of agency in analysis of the welfare state. *Critical Social Policy*. Spring Issue

Marris, P. (1987). *Meaning and Action*. London: Routledge and Kegan Paul

Martin, I. S. (1992.) New times: new directions. *Community Education Network*. 12(9)

Mayo, M. (1994). *Communities and Caring: The Mixed Economy of Welfare*, Basingstoke: Macmillan

Meekosha, H. (1993). The bodies politic – equality, difference and community practice. *In:* H. Butcher et al, eds. *Community and Public Policy*. London: Pluto Press in assoc. with Community Development Foundation and Bradford and Ilkley College

Miller, C. and Bryant, R. (1990). Community work in the UK: reflections on the 1980s. *Community Development Journal*. 25(3)

Milliband, R. (1994). *Socialism for a Sceptical Age*. Polity Press

Morris, J. (1991/92). Us and them? Feminist research, community care and disability. *Critical Social Policy*. Issue 33

Oliver, M. (1990). *The Politics of Disablement*. Basingstoke: Macmillan

Stuart, M. and Thompson, D. (1995). *Engaging with Difference – The 'Other' in Adult Education*. NIACE

Tudor, K. (1990/92). One step back, two steps forward: community care and mental health. *Critical Social Policy*. Winter Issue

Walmsley, S. (1993). Contradictions in caring: reciprocity and interdependence. *Disability, Handicap and Society*. 8(2)

Wolfensberger, W. (1972). *Normalization*. Toronto: NIMR

Chapter 7: Disabled People and Inclusion: A Discourse of Rights, not Charity

Margaret Petrie

Synopsis

All too often community work regards disability issues as the preserve of social work. The author argues, however, that the pursuit of social justice, which is implicit in the radical project, must recognise that experience of structural inequality places disabled people within the same disadvantaging power relationships as other oppressed groups which have traditionally made up the constituency of community work.

The inequalities, which are implicit in both formal and informal education sectors, are intensifying in a marketised system. Nevertheless the chapter makes the case for improved access for disabled people in a way which goes beyond the 'additive' approach which characterises so much 'special' education provision. Grounding her analysis in the social model of disability, and the effects of 'the disabling society', the author argues for the rights and entitlements of disabled people as equal citizens. In contrast, 'special needs' or 'integration' imply personal deficiency, and are aimed at adaptation rather than change.

The oppression of disabled people must be located in wider social and cultural relations of power. The chapter, therefore, recognises that the exclusion of disabled people is a fundamental contradiction of any concept of anti-discriminatory or inclusive practice. The author advocates an approach which sees structural and cultural barriers as its key target and solidarity in difference as its key aspiration.

Introduction

Recently we have seen the introduction of legislation which claims to facilitate the more effective integration of disabled children and adults into our schools, colleges and communities. Such legislation is defined in terms of 'Caring for People' (1989) or meeting 'special educational needs' HMSO (1980), a discourse which implies a very particular view of disabled people as those who need to be cared for and who are 'special' or 'different'. It is notable that the Civil Rights Bill tabled by Roger Berry in 1994 which used, instead, the language of entitlement was defeated in parliament and a greatly watered-down version – 'The Disability Discrimination Act' (1995) is now on the statute book. The Disability Movement's struggle to gain Civil Rights for disabled people and the publicity they have achieved via direct action initiatives has been successful in generating recognition that discrimination against disabled people exists and is unacceptable. Local Authorities, waking up to the fact that they have been responsible for discriminating against disabled people, have begun to develop policies for integration in schools and in the Community Education Service. How do we ensure, however, that this seemingly knee-jerk reaction does not become little more than a cosmetic exercise?

Integration or inclusion – what's in a word?

Integration has not always been a positive experience for disabled people, particularly when it involves attempts by non disabled people to assist them to slot more effectively into fixed educational or social settings where their requirements may only be partially met or not at all. With demands for inclusion rather than integration, Organisations of Disabled People are attempting to draw a distinction between 'integration', which implies that disabled people adapt to a fixed educational and social structure, and 'inclusion', which demands the restructuring of educational settings and communities to accommodate diversity and difference (Mason 1994). In the same way that women, black people and gay and lesbian people have insisted that institutionalised sexism, racism and homophobia be brought to the surface and confronted openly, disabled people are demanding that disability be recognised, not as an individualised difficulty, but as a social creation.

It is notable that disabled peoples' struggles against discrimination have rarely rated a mention in community work literature. Disability issues, it seems, have been regarded as the responsibility of social work. Writers such as Baldock (1983), for example, have pointed out that community workers have been keen to distance themselves from the so called 'caring' professions which may be associated with individualised explanations of social problems. Community workers are quick to define themselves as those who work alongside or with people – not those who work for or on them. It is significant, then, that on the rare occasions that disabled people do feature in the literature, it is often in the context of their relationship as 'dependants' of others. Baldock's article, which argues for Community Development approaches to Community Care, for example, concentrates on the concerns of the carers of 'those who stand in special need of care'. Disabled people are the 'acted on' – not those who can act of and for themselves.

Jenny Morris (1991) has pointed out that feminist concerns about women's role as carers has often failed to recognise the interests of women who are also the recipients of 'care'. This 'them and us' mentality has led to analyses such as Gillian Dalley's (1988) argument for 'collective forms of care' as the only means by which women can free themselves from the social burden of caring. The right of disabled women to choose how and where they live is ignored in favour of the interests of non disabled women who, presumably, will always remain non disabled! (see Shaw in this volume)

By assuming that disability issues are solely a social welfare concern, we are in danger of tacitly accepting an analysis of disability which sees disabled people as those who need to be cured or cared for. In this account individual impairment is identified as the reason why disabled people do not participate on an equal basis with others in society. However if we substituted the words 'individual impairment' with gender, skin colour or sexuality and the words 'disabled people' with women, black or gay people the connection with other forms of oppression can easily be made.

This chapter argues for a clear analysis of disability which recognises it as a social creation, which repositions disabled people from their traditional position of 'object' ('acted on') to 'subject' ('actor') and which locates disabled people not at the edge but at the centre of radical community work practice. Community workers have much to learn from disability politics and disabled people because they challenge us once again to consider our own prejudices, to reconsider our approaches to community development, to educational practice and to define just what we mean by equal opportunities and anti-discriminatory practice.

This chapter will look firstly at models of disability drawing mainly on the writing of disability activists. It will explore the effects of marketisation on the context within which we are working, the contradictions inherent in current funding arrangements, issues of access and, in relation to these issues, the role of the community worker.

The medical model of disability

Historically, disability has been defined by medical conditions such as spina bifida, epilepsy, polio, and so on. The medical model of disability is one which, fundamentally, views the person with an impairment as having something 'wrong' with them which has to be 'cured'. Of course many impairments cannot be cured and, in this process, those concerned are labelled as 'deficient', somehow 'less than' others. Operating within this model, the medical profession has striven to cure, repair or remove the impairment in order to 'normalise' the person. This approach implies – albeit unconsciously – a philosophy, which emphasises the survival of the fittest and the belief that 'defects' can be bred out. The more extreme end of this social eugenics continuum, of which Hitler was a supporter can, at worst, justify the horrifying vision of Nazi Germany and it's programme for 'the destruction of unworthy life' which sanctioned the execution of 80 - 100,000 disabled people.

This deficit model of disability is confirmed by the commonplace practice of social segregation which has included placing disabled children in special or residential schools which are outside their community, and dividing people according to their medical condition such as 'schools for spastics' or 'blind schools'. In adult life disabled people are offered sheltered employment, day centres or the social isolation of home confinement. This is compounded by barriers such as the lack of access to public space, transport, buildings or the lack of information in formats other than standard print. It is this lack of access, this social segregation, this attitude that disabled people are defective that the disability movement defines as 'the disabling society'.

The disabling society

Influential writers in the Disability Movement such as Finkelstein (1993), Oliver (1990) and Rieser and Mason (1991) have represented the argument that disability is a social creation, using the undisputable force of practical example:

'All disabled people experience disability as social restriction, whether those restrictions occur as a consequence of inaccessible built environments, questionable notions of intelligence and social competence, the inability of the general population to use sign language, the lack of reading material in Braille or hostile public attitudes to people with non visible disabilities'. (Oliver 1990)

This model of disability, known as the Social Model, has been developed by disabled people in opposition to individualising medical analyses which define their *particular* impairment as the chief barrier to full participation in society. In 1981, International Year for Disabled People, Disabled Peoples' International was formed, the first coming together of people with different types of impairment from around the world, speaking with a united voice – expressing the views of the 10% of the world's population who are disabled in one respect or another. Disabled Peoples' International came up with this brief definition:

'Disability is the loss or limitation of opportunities to take part in the normal life of the community on an equal level with others due to physical or social barriers'. (Dreidger 1989)

Writers such as Shakespeare (1994), Morris (1991) and Crow (1992) have offered analyses of disability which aim to develop the social model further, drawing on parallels with feminist theory. Whilst Crow warns against ignoring the, sometimes painful, reality of individual lived experience, Shakespeare argues that in rejecting the 'individual medical tragedy theory' of disability in favour of sociological explanations, it is important not to ignore 'questions of culture, representation and meaning' in understanding disability. He argues that disabled people's negative representation in books, plays, television and in the press serves a purpose for non disabled people:

' ... disabled people become ciphers for those feelings, processes or characteristics with which non disabled society cannot deal .... Disabled people enable non disabled people to feel good about themselves: by demeaning disabled people, non-disabled people can feel powerful and generous. Disabled people, on the other hand are viewed as objects of pity and of aid' (ibid. 1994).

He draws similarities, here, with the representation in charity campaigns of black people from developing countries. He also makes a comparison between the objectification of women and that of disabled people, where each are represented as a passive and available body to be stared at. As Morris (1991) puts it:

'It is not only physical limitations that restrict us to our homes and those that we know. It is the knowledge that each entry into the public world will be dominated by stares, by condescension, by pity and by hostility'.

She also points to the fact that the non disabled population's fears and wish to deny their own frailty, vulnerability and mortality encourages a desire to distance or separate themselves from disabled people, to define them as 'other or 'not like us'. Shakespeare (1994) further argues:

'Disabled people are scapegoats. It is not just that disabled people are different, expensive, inconvenient or odd: it is that they represent a threat – either to order, or, to the self conception of western human beings – who since the Enlightenment have viewed themselves as perfectible, as all knowing, as god-like: able, over and above all other beings, to conquer the limitations of their nature through victories of their culture'.

Some argue, however, that policy developments in the form of anti discrimination legislation, mainstream education for a growing number of disabled children, a statutory obligation on colleges to offer provision to students with 'learning difficulties' (a term which applies to students with physical, sensory and learning impairments) and Community Care legislation with its stated emphasis on independent living heralds a fundamental shift in attitudes and a closing of the gap in terms of equal opportunities. These developments have, however, to be put in the context of the increasing marketisation of public services including education and an emphasis on reducing the burden of the state.

Educational access, competition and community care

A series of legislation has been enacted aiming to introduce competition and market forces into educational provision, justified in the language of 'freedom' and 'opportunity' and claiming to improve standards and increase consumer choice. The Education Reform Act (1988), for example, gave schools the opportunity to 'opt out' of local authority control and to become self governing. The Further and Higher Education (Scotland) Act (1992) similarly removed colleges from local authority control. School pupils and students were to become 'consumers' in the 'free market' of educational provision. School league tables of exam results were introduced to allow parents to decide in which school their child would be most likely to achieve good results, and to create competition between schools. Under the Parents Charter, parents were given the option of sending their children to a school outside their catchment area. Despite the much-heralded emphasis on parental control and choice, however, this right was not extended to parents of disabled children wishing to send their children to mainstream rather than special schools. Despite the 1981 Education Act which was intended to facilitate the integration of more disabled children into mainstream schools, the number of children in 'special' schools in 1989 was less than one percent lower than it was in 1977 (BCODP, 1991).

Educational policy in recent years has been couched in terms of investing in people. The social investment argument is developed in the political Right's assertion that education should address demands for an appropriately-trained workforce who can meet the needs of industry, thereby improving economic efficiency. What this assumes, of course, is that the needs of industry and the needs of society coincide. The fact, for example, that disabled people are 'consistently three times more likely to be out of work and unemployed for longer periods than non disabled people according to government figures' (BCODP 1991) somewhat undermines such a claim. It also denies the fact that our society is heterogeneous and that different interest groups may have conflicting aspirations. The emphasis on the needs of industry does underline, however, the economic motivation underpinning much recent legislation.

The stated aims of Community Care, outlined in the Caring for People White Paper (1989) were to 'enable people to live as normal a life as possible in their own homes or in a homely environment in the local community', 'to provide the right amount of care and support to help people achieve maximum possible independence ... to achieve their full potential' and 'to give people a greater individual say in how they live their lives and the services they need to help them do so'. However, a recent survey by Scope (1995) found that Care in the Community had largely failed to deliver the user-controlled, needs-led services originally promised by the Griffiths report (HMSO 1988) and the subsequent White Paper. Instead, a recent High court decision ruled that social services can take their own resources into account when assessing a person's need for community care services – a clear indication that community care is not needs, but funding led.

The White Paper also states that 'promoting choice and independence underlies all the Government's proposals.' Such rhetoric, however, ignores the existence of differential access to economic resources and power. Choice does not, of course, exist in a vacuum. Choice will undoubtedly be affected by social and economic factors. A person who uses a wheelchair, for example, cannot 'choose' to take up the opportunity of a place in an educational institution which is inaccessible to wheelchair users. A person who requires personal assistance to go to the toilet cannot 'choose' to live independently unless they have the resources to employ personal assistants. Without the necessary financial and practical resources, then, a shift to disabled people living in their own homes does not imply independence but simply another form of dependence on relatives and, specifically, women. As Morris (1991) points out, disabled people and their organisations view the provision and control over personal assistance as a human rights issue, rejecting 'the way in which disabled and older people are forced to look for support from their relatives and partners .... We should receive the financial support we require to enable us to make free choices about the kind of personal assistance we require'.

Whilst the introduction of the Independent Living Fund to the UK in 1988 has meant this has begun to be a possibility for some people, the tightening up of benefit regulations equally consigns many people to isolation, poverty and a mutually-inhibiting dependence on relatives. Similarly, whilst the use of new technology and the funding made available by the Disabled Students' Allowance has meant that some disabled people are able to compete effectively with non-disabled people on mainstream education courses, they may still, however, find themselves isolated from the social aspects of student life due to basics such as inaccessible public transport. In other words, what is given in a limited way with one hand is taken away on a grand scale with the other.

In addition, those institutions that are accessible will often offer provision specifically for disabled people either in a college solely for people with disabilities or in a mainstream institution. Either way disabled people often find themselves segregated once again into courses which are specifically designed for them, such as Lifeskills or Extension courses which can lead onto Youth Training but from there, often, nowhere. The justification for this effective apartheid is often given on the basis that disabled young people frequently leave school without the entry qualifications necessary to access more mainstream courses. This, of course, raises questions about the nature of education being offered in the first place. As highlighted earlier, the dominant medical model of disability assumes that disabled people will always need to be cured or cared for. Without education, which allows disabled children and young people to reach their full potential, this often becomes a self-fulfilling prophecy.

Some colleges are attempting to offer bridges to mainstream courses with the introduction of certification of the achievements of 'students with learning difficulties' and many hope that the introduction of anti-discrimination legislation will lead to greater employment opportunities (Dumbleton 1995). Disabled people currently undertaking courses, however, have few employment opportunities to move on to and may either end up in a Day Centre or on a merry-go-round of different courses which do not progress anywhere. It is encouraging that disability issues are moving higher up the educational agenda – Higher Education institutions in Scotland have just received funding from the Scottish Higher Education Funding Council for specialist equipment to make their institutions more accessible to people with disabilities and to employ Disability Advisors based in their institutions. The problem is, however, that disabled people are still seen to be an 'add on', a special group for whom additional resources must be provided. As in the case of community care, the focus is on the disabled person 'fitting in'. The disabled student is still identified as a problem which needs to be solved.

Disability activists have highlighted a common source of oppression – those attitudes which identify disabled people as separate, as 'other'. This concept is translated, in educational policy, into 'special' educational needs and, therefore, a necessity for 'special' provision. The implicit assumption is, once again, 'them and us' (see Shaw in this volume). Provision for disabled people, in this account, is defined in terms of disabled people's perceived inadequacies. The underlying philosophy is, again, the medical model of disability which essentially views impairment as the problem.

Jonathon (1985 and 1990) has pointed out that, at the heart of recent Conservative educational policy, is the notion that individuals should have the freedom to pursue their own rational self-interest. She argues, however, that within a competitive framework one individual interest must operate at the expense of another which may not, ultimately, benefit the majority, much less those whose unequal starting position place them at a considerable disadvantage in the first place. In addition, even in the unlikely event that a disabled person can attend the educational institution of their choice, they have no freedom of choice concerning the nature or content of the education they will receive when they get there. What, then, are the implications for curriculum?

Access to what?

Government has devolved control for the management of schools and colleges at the same time as they have maintained control over the content of the curriculum; by the introduction of a national curriculum in schools, and the imposition of a strict emphasis on vocationalism in colleges. In this context education is being defined solely as 'training for work'. This current emphasis on vocationalism in education was spawned in the 1970s by the Black Papers which argued that the post-war aim of education to offer equality of opportunity, to only discriminate on grounds of merit and so to achieve greater social equality had failed, evidenced by rising youth unemployment and, it was claimed, a lowering of social and moral standards (Ball, 1990). Young people were leaving school ill-equipped to deal with a changing labour market. Unemployment, therefore, was the result of inappropriate education. The Thatcher government was also able to capitalise on public opinion that educational policy, which had claimed to create equality of opportunity, had failed for the majority of its participants. Meanwhile, disabled people had rarely even been given the chance to compete in the race.

In addition, notions of individual opportunity and vocationalism do have some currency for the education 'consumer'. Most of us, of course, engage in education because of its potential exchange value on the labour market. People want to do courses which will ultimately lead to employment. Disabled people are, of course, no different from anyone else in this respect. A survey by OPCS indicated that, whilst two-thirds of all disabled people do not work, approximately half of this number wanted to work – given the right circumstances (Gooding 1994).

Jonathon (1985) points out, however, that education cannot, on its own, achieve social change without concomitant changes in the social structure. A wrong diagnosis therefore leads to the wrong prescription. Education, even vocational education, cannot of itself create employment. The choices people have will depend on the vagaries of the employment market and the perceived demand for specific skills will, in turn, have an impact on the courses available. The choices available to disabled people will also be crucially affected by the pressure on employers to be 'cost effective' and their perceptions of whether a disabled person can work as effectively as a non disabled person.

Education policy emphasising the opportunity for all to achieve on their own merits denies the fact that, in a competitive social framework, there must be winners and losers and that the odds are unfairly stacked against some people at the start of the race. For example, the National Curriculum demands that students must now acquire specific competences to a nationally agreed standard in order to achieve the positive outcome of a vocational qualification. This implies that all student progress can be measured on the basis of uniform standards of assessment. At first glance this might seem like a fair system except, of course that all students are not the same, do not learn in the same way or at the same rate and do not have the same starting positions. Disabled people cannot equally or fairly compete in an educational framework which is currently designed to militate against difference. A national curriculum with an emphasis on competence in certain tasks is predicated on the existence of an unequal social structure in which the survival of the fittest, quickest, sharpest or indeed richest is all.

Educational integration, therefore, often means attempting to slot disabled people into an educational framework in which they will inevitably be found 'deficient' when assessed against some spurious notion of the 'average' student. This of course is an issue which does not just effect disabled people. A competitive educational framework has, arguably, led to a considerable number of pupils and students leaving education with an indelible sense of their own failure. Further, a national curriculum treats knowledge as an ideologically neutral commodity which can be handed out like so many bowls of rice. Paulo Freire (1972) argues:

> 'There is no such thing as a neutral education process. Education either functions as an instrument which is used to facilitate the integration of the younger generation into the logic of the present system and bring about conformity to it or it becomes the practice of freedom the means by which men and women deal critically and creatively with reality and discover how to participate in the transformation of their world.'

This point is underlined by the invisibility of disabled people in the educational curriculum. Where they do appear they are often defined in the form of some broad stereotypes: the 'tragic but brave' victim of circumstance as represented in the popular press, the superhuman disabled person who individually overcomes their impairment to achieve their goals (aren't they wonderful!) such as Douglas Bader, or the frightening, evil, sinister person whose impairment is an illustration of their inner wickedness and cruelty, such as Captain Hook or Long John Silver. This latter representation is a particularly insidious one, featuring frequently in popular culture such as children's books and cartoons where the 'baddies' are often people with disfigurement or impairment, such as in Batman or Dick Tracy.

Oliver and Barnes (1991) point out that disabled people are socialised into dependency, particularly because the special education system instils passivity. They highlight one study which found that disabled young people 'appear to have been conditioned into accepting a devalued role as sick, pitiful and a burden of charity' (Hutchison and Tennyson in Oliver and Barnes 1991). Barnes further argues:

'Institutional discrimination against disabled people is ingrained throughout the present educational system. This data shows that most of the educational provision for disabled children and students remains basically segregative, is dominated by traditionally medically influenced attitudes and commands low priority as a whole. As a result, rather than equipping disabled children and young people with appropriate skills and opportunities to live a full life, it largely conditions them to accepting much devalued social roles and in doing so condemns them to a lifetime of dependence and subordination'.

With their demands for inclusive education, disabled people and their organisations are demanding, not only an end to the damaging segregation of disabled people, but also a restructuring of educational curriculum and practice to take account of difference. How then might this impact on the practice of community work?

Community work and inclusion

Keddie (1980) has argued that one of the main themes of adult education has been to 'take a better kind of education to those whose previous education has been misconceived'. She suggests, however, that adult education frequently mirrors the competitive emphasis on individual achievement that is prevalent in school education. Similarly, community workers may frequently find themselves in the contradictory role of recognising that the social system is problematic, but engaged in a process of enabling people to adapt to that system. Frequently the way we are funded encourages this approach. My employing agency, Access Ability Lothian, for example, is funded to work specifically with disabled people because they are identified as a disadvantaged group. By focusing the funding on disabled people as victims the implication is that it is neither educational provision nor the social structure which has to change but, rather, disabled people themselves. They just need additional support. In this context, therefore, the discourse is one of deficiency, not discrimination.

Drawing on Foucault's concept of 'discourse' – that is that the way we talk about the world and the way we experience it are inextricably linked – Oliver (1993) argues that the language of 'caring' associated with welfare provision and applied to disabled people is in direct contradiction to the language of rights and obligations associated with active citizenship. He quotes Ignatieff:

> 'The language of citizenship is not properly about compassion at all, since compassion is a private virtue which cannot be legislated or enforced. The practice of citizenship is about ensuring everyone has the entitlements necessary to the exercise of their liberty. As a political question, welfare is about rights, not caring and the history of citizenship has been the struggle to make freedom real not to tie us all in the leading strings of therapeutic good intentions'.

Disability issues, then, are not merely a question of 'care' but represent a familiar site of struggle against poverty, inequality and discrimination. The question for community education workers is how they support or inhibit this struggle.

A crucial first step is recognising that non disabled people cannot define *for* disabled people what they need. Access Ability Lothian, for example, is managed by disabled people. The fact that disabled people are in control working with a shared understanding of the nature of their own oppression represents, in itself, a challenge to the ideology which views disabled people only as dependent. In the same way that it has been important for women, black people, gay and lesbian people, part of the wider political struggle of disabled people for civil rights has been to create and control their own organisations – to represent their own interests. Community workers who wish to make their provision more accessible must, therefore, first consult disabled people since they are the best experts about the social and practical barriers which prevent them accessing local resources.

Removing physical barriers, providing information in various formats and offering human and practical aids to communication are all important steps in breaking down barriers to inclusion. These things, of course, cost money and inadequate resourcing is frequently used as a reason to exclude disabled people. The Government baulked at the Civil Rights Bill because they said it would cost too much. In addition to the questionable nature of the Government's figures (Gooding 1994b), the skewed logic of the argument is that it is reasonable to design public space, buildings, and transport which excludes part of the population. Disabled people are not merely an additional extra. They are an intrinsic part of the community. Access is, furthermore, an issue for parents of young children, elderly people and for people experiencing temporary ill health or injury.

The danger in these 'New Times', when we are asked to reject 'grand theories' such as Marxism and feminism – which are considered too totalising and which do not take enough account of diversity and difference – is that we translate this into a fragmented approach to community work practice which implicitly ignores the commonalities in different forms of oppression. The community work constituency is often segregated, both conceptually and actually, into special interest or identity groups: unemployed men, disabled people, women, ethnic minorities, elderly people and so on. Meekosha (1993) uses the phrase 'managing diversity' to describe the way in which governments respond to the demands of identity groups whilst simultaneously constructing neat categories in an attempt to maintain harmonious social relations. She points out:

> 'As community work becomes increasingly moulded by the pressures of market models of welfare, the historic focus of community work as a profession of activism and commitment to the achievement of social justice becomes translated. It has now become a mode of work in which ever more tightly delineated minorities and sectors of society experiencing discrimination are channelled into organising the provision of specific usually volunteer-operated services.'

In questioning how we deal with some of the contradictions of current practice, she suggests: 'The important task may not be constructing unity, but achieving solidarity from the vantage point of our difference.'

An inclusive practice, then, is one which, whilst acknowledging diversity and difference, does not segregate people according to 'special' categories. It starts from the understanding that we are all special, all different; and designs the educational provision to fulfil the requirements of all community members. It is not, then, a question of regarding disabled people as an additional extra, but of recognising that the exclusion of disabled people is a fundamental contradiction to any concept of anti-discriminatory or inclusive practice.

Acting in solidarity with disabled people means recognising the social context of disabled people's individual oppression and challenging the structural and cultural forces which seek to maintain it. It means supporting and encouraging their demands for inclusion and exposing the attitudinal and practical barriers which stand in their way. It also means being willing to fight segregation within our own work places and institutions. This process requires us to confront our own prejudices and fear and our own limited perceptions of what disabled people can and cannot do. We also need to recognise that disability issues are not only issues for disabled people, but part of the process of institutional discrimination which sustains widespread social inequality. Disabled people's struggles for civil rights can be linked to similar struggles in the trade union movement, the women's movement and the black civil rights movement.

When potentially progressive integration or community care legislation is introduced without appropriate funding it can quickly come to be seen as regressive. Without a theoretical analysis we can fall into the trap of blaming the principle rather than the practice. For instance, the fact that legislation or policy which promotes and facilitates integration may be badly planned and under resourced does not vindicate, as is sometimes argued, those who wish to maintain segregation (see McGill and Theakstone 1994). Martin (1987) argues that 'the theory and practice of community education must be continuously reconstructed to reflect and engage with the changing social reality of the community'. I would argue that, central to that 'continuous reconstruction', community workers must be clear about both their theoretical and practical position regarding disabled people. By adapting Martin's analytical models of community education, I would like to draw a distinction between community work practice informed by the medical model of disability and that informed by the social model (see table 1).

Table 1. Models of Community Work in relation to Disability
(adapted from Martin 1987)

	Medical Model	*Social Model*
Implicit model of society/community	Consensus	Conflict
Premise	Impairment problematic defined as "other"	Society's response to impairment, problematic celebration of difference
Strategy	Special educational needs provision Integration	Self Advocacy/disability led groups, challenging barriers to inclusion
Initial focus	Segregated schools/ courses Day Centres	Local disability action groups, disability studies ensuring accessibility, incorporation of disability issues into curriculum
Key Influences	Medical Profession	Disability Movement, V. Finkelstein, M. Mason, R. Rieser, M. Oliver, J. Morris, C. Barnes
Twentieth-cent. origins	Social Eugenics Movement	Organisations of Disabled Peoples' International
Dominant Themes	Homogeniety	Existing provision problematic
	Decompartmentalization	Structural/cultural analysis
	Rehabilitation	Disability equality/ political education
	Normalisation	Solidarity and alliances
	Neutrality	User control
	Charity	Personal is political
	"We know best"	Rights
	Curing/caring	Citizenship
Organisation	Top down (professional leadership) Formal Institution Programme Reactive	Bottom up (user-led) Informal Process Proactive

Conclusion

Community workers have clear choices to make: either we discriminate or we do not. If, for example, we devise our practice around non-disabled people, with disabled people as an afterthought, then we are discriminating. If, however, we plan and implement every aspect of our service, taking account of the different requirements of *all* our potential participants, only then are we engaging in non-discriminatory practice. Meekosha (1993) suggests we should see ourselves as 'a profession committed to activism and the achievement of social justice'. We have to be careful that the actions we take along the way don't contradict this long term goal.

Acknowledgement

I would like to thank Sue Pearson and Neil Robinson for their assistance in writing this article

References

Baldock, P. (1983). Community development and community care. *In: Community Work Level 2, Selected Reading.* 1992

Ball, S. (1990). *Politics and Policy Making in Education: Explorations in Policy Sociology.* Routledge

Barnes, C. (1991). *Disabled People in Britain and Discrimination: A Case for Anti-Discrimination Legislation.* C. Hurst and Co.

British Council of Organisations of Disabled People, (1991): Disabled People and Institutional Discrimination, BCODP

Caring for People, Community Care in the Next Decade and Beyond 1989: HMSO

Crow, L. (1992). Renewing the social model of disability. *Coalition.* July

Dalley, G. (1988). *Collectivism Defined in Ideologies of Caring: Rethinking Community and Collectivism.* Macmillan

Dreidger. (1989). *The Last Civil Rights Movements.* Hurst, London

Dumbleton P. (1995). "Becoming Visible: A Review of Current Developments in Special Programmes in Scottish Further Education." *Educare, Skill* (National Bureau for Students with Disabilities). March

Education (Scotland) Act (1980). Chapter 44. London: HMSO

Finkelstein, V. (1993). *Disabling Barriers – Enabling Environments.* Open University and Sage Publications

Freire, P. (1972). *Pedagogy of the Oppressed.* Penguin

Gooding, C. (1994a). *Disabling Laws, Enabling Acts: Disability Rights in Britain and America.* Pluto Press

Gooding, C. (1994b). *What Price Civil Rights, The Facts Behind the Myths of the Cost Compliance Assessment.* Rights Now Campaign, 12 City Forum, 250 City Road, London ECIV 8AF

HMSO. (1988). The Griffiths Reports: Community Caree: An Agenda for Action

Jonathon, R. (1985). Education and 'The Needs of Society'. *In: A.* Hartnett and M. Naish, eds. *Education and Society Today.* Falmer Press

Jonathon, R. (1990). State education service or prisoners dilemma: the 'hidden hand' as source of education policy. *British Journal of Educational Studies.* 38(2), May

Keddie, N. (1980). Adult education: an ideology of individualism. *In:* J. L. Thompson, ed. *Adult Education for a Change.* Hutchison

Martin, I. (1987). Community education: towards a theoretical analysis. *In:* Allen, Bastiani, Martin and Richards, eds. *Community Education: An Agenda for Educational Reform.* Open University Press 1987

McGill and Theakstone (1994). Special school – a positive choice. *Disability News.* Autumn

Meekosha, H. (1993). The bodies politic – equality, difference and community practice. *In:* Butcher et al, eds. *Community and Public Policy.* London: Pluto Press in assoc. with Community Development Foundation and Bradford and Ilkley College

Morris, J. (1991). *Pride Against Prejudice: Transforming Attitudes to Disability.* The Women's Press

Oliver, M. (1990). *The Politics of Disablement.* MacMillan

Oliver, M. (1993). OU Course K665 The Disabling Society, Workbook 2 Disability, Citizenship and Empowerment. The Open University

Oliver, M. (1988). The social and political context of educational policy: the case of special needs. *In:* L. Barton, ed. *The Politics of Special Educational Needs.* Falmer Press

Oliver, M. and Barnes, C. (1991). Discrimination, disability and welfare : from needs to rights. *In:* Swain, French, Finkelstein and Oliver, eds. *Disabling Barriers – Enabling Environments.* Sage Publications in association with Open University

Rieser, R. and Mason M. (1991). *Disability equality in the classroom: a human rights issue.* Disability Equality in Education, London

Rieser, R. and Mason M. (1993). *Altogether Better (from 'Special Needs' to Equality in Education).* Comic Relief

Shakespeare, T. (1994). Cultural representation of disabled people: dustbins for disavowal? *Disability and Society.* 9(3)

Chapter 8: Domestication or Liberation? Working-class Women and Community Work Practice

Jane Meagher and Lyn Tett

Synopsis

In this chapter the authors consider the relationship between women, work, class and community work practice. They argue that the ideologies which community workers espouse and the funding regimes within which they operate have a crucial effect on practice. Community work can be either domesticating or liberating. Unless community workers critically examine their practice, the former is more likely than the latter because unconscious assumptions and reactions reproduce the everyday practices of an economically and socially divided society.

Focusing on working class women, they advocate a practice which treats women as subjects of their own learning, and for a definition of class which is not reductionist – recognising that class position is always mediated by other identities. Radical community work practice can be seen as a way of catalysing the diversity of people's lived experience with solidarity through an understanding of oppression at both local and global levels.

Introduction

In 1980 the United Nations pointed out that 'women represent 50% of the adult world population and one third of the official labour force, they [work] for nearly two-thirds of all working hours for which they receive only one-tenth of the world income: but they own less than 1% of the world property'. In 1990 Oppenheim argued 'there is nothing new about women's poverty …. At the start of this century 61% of adults in the United Kingdom on all forms of poor relief were women …. Today 62% of adults supported by Income Support are women'. The 1994 Gender Audit summarised the position of women in the labour market in Scotland thus: 'the majority of women in employment work in low-paid, low-grade jobs, in the service sector of the economy; over 40% work part-time; on average women's pay is just over two-thirds of men's' (p12). This latter figure is likely to be a considerable under-estimation of the true state of affairs since the New Earnings Survey data exclude those who earn below the tax threshold (see Scottish Low Pay Unit, 1994).

Women and Work

In trying to understand women's poor economic position and their predominance in part-time, temporary, low-paid jobs in the service sector in the United Kingdom, three broad explanations have been suggested. These are:-

1)   that women's circumstances as the main carers for children and adults mean that they prefer part-time, monotonous jobs because this enables them to combine this work with their 'family responsibilities' and, because they have access to sufficient support beyond their own earnings, they are at best only partially committed to waged labour:

2)   that job segregation by gender means that some types of work are labelled as 'for women', and because women have little power they are denied access to better paid employment. Women earn less than men even when their jobs have objectively equivalent requirements for education, experience, skill and working conditions (see Gaskell, 1992):

3)   that the general characteristics of women's work, as part-time, intermittent, low-paid and unprotected by labour regulations, act as mechanisms for producing and keeping a subordinated and relatively powerless work-force. In other words these are coercive mechanisms of labour discipline.

Perhaps all these explanations can be combined to show how, what Hart (1992) has called the 'housewifisation' of labour, has come about. She argues that in the market economy it is the cheapness of labour which has gained primacy in economic performance. She says:-

'The housewife, whose work is (ideally) entirely free of charge, must inevitably become the ideal form of labour, representing the highest degree of cheapness. Housewifised labour, therefore, has two major dimensions: it is socially devalued, and it is associated with the idea that the cheap labourers have somehow access to resources outside the wage relation to cover their subsistence' (p26).

Currently, the service sector represents by far the largest growth in female employment in the United Kingdom and is likely to account for most of the predicted growth in women's participation in the labour force. This sector has a low capital-to-labour ratio and operates in a highly competitive environment which encourages employment practices which depress wage levels and require work-forces which can be expanded or contracted in relation to fluctuations in demand. So what is required is both a cheap and flexible work-force.

It is no accident, we contend, that this work-force is overwhelmingly female. Employers single out women because they are able to take advantage of their weak and vulnerable economic and social position and justify this by arguing that they are seeking 'feminine skills' such as dexterity and that low wages are appropriate because it is only a 'contribution' to the household income. Because money is seen to equate with social status and power, women's free labour in the home becomes a way of reducing their access to full membership in society. As Bennholdt-Thomsen (1984:254) points out 'to be a housewife is not a decision women make but an image that persecutes women like an infectious disease'.

This image of women seems to us to have the power to show not only why women predominate in the part-time, low-paid employment sectors but also why men are virtually absent. In addition, essentialist notions of women as being 'naturally' more suited to caring for children and elders justifies both their predominance in the 'caring' sector of employment, and expectations that they are the gender that will have responsibility for these groups in the private sphere (see Shaw in this volume). The male hierarchical ordering of society, which is preserved through marriage and the family via the sexual division of labour, ensures that women are the group that lose out at home and at work.

Women and Class

The current political context suggests that inequalities arising out of class differences have largely disappeared and that we live in John Major's 'classless society'. Does community work practice accept that class oppression no longer exists or are we, through our policies and practices, colluding in the silencing of working class people and in the denial of their experiences? In what ways do we take into account the history and changing economic activities of working class women as well as their points of contact with the feminist movement?

Goldthorpe and Marshall (1992) argue that if it were true that, as some claim, class has ceased to be a factor in British society, then there would be an observable movement away from a 'closed' class society towards a meritocratic society of a more open kind. However, their research finds little evidence for such fluidity and they conclude that 'There is in fact no reason to suppose that over recent decades, classes in Britain, the working class included, have shown any weakening in their social cohesion or their ideological distinctiveness'. (p391)

Community work has made its own contribution to the view that class no longer exists. A survey of the language used – the disadvantaged, the poor, the deprived, the needy and so on – reveals the liberal underpinnings that inform, consciously or unconsciously, the principles and practice of the Community Education Service in Scotland. Westwood (1992) for example, traces historical moves in adult education away from its more radical roots towards 'community' and the almost imperceptible removal of class from the adult education agenda. In its work with women, community work has embraced this liberal discourse and is thus concerned with equality of opportunity, access to the job market and to further and higher education, or mere domestication in the form of aerobics and sewing classes (see, for example, Hughes 1993; Tett 1994). This analysis tends to ignore any conflict of interest between working class and middle class women and fails to tackle the economic roots of women's oppression, denying working class women a link into their own history and interests through a totalising analysis which subsumes diversity and shifting definitions of identity by assuming the homogeneity of 'sisterhood' (see Meekosha 1993).

It has to be acknowledged that fights for equality by women have exposed some of the vested interests of the white, male-dominated power structures of the organised labour movement. Cockburn (1983) provides ample illustration of the ways in which men in the newspaper industry in London used work and technology to maintain their power over women. The labour movement has traditionally tended to ignore or marginalise the struggles of women in the workplace (for example during the strike by black women at the Imperial Typewriter factory in Leicester in the 1970s).

The move away from traditional working class occupations in heavy industry, the introduction of new technologies, the decline of the regions and cultures associated with the old manufacturing base, the increase in the service industries, the introduction of a more part-time, flexible and largely female workforce to meet the needs of international capital, have all combined to challenge the assumptions and traditions of the labour movement. The question is whether, fundamentally, all these changes are bringing about the death throes of class, or whether, as Sivanandan (1992) argues, capitalism is merely regrouping – breaking down the old barriers and rebuilding new ones. In this sense it is women who now form part of the new working class – class cleansed of gender assumptions, of racist and cultural stereotypes, and restated as a relationship of systematic economic exploitation.

In summary, a picture emerges of working class women cut off from traditional sites of class struggle and recruited into part-time, low-paid, non-unionised occupations, historically defined in class terms only in relation to men and living in a climate that tells them that class does not exist any more. That these structural and structured elements of women's experience are often ignored by community work practice compounds the situation.

Women's Work

The dominant paradigm within the Local Authority funded Community Education Service in Scotland is implicitly 'reformist' because it is assumed that resources are there for the taking once groups have learnt how to access them (see Martin 1993). The Service therefore sees its role as positively advantaging 'disadvantaged' groups and 'deprived' areas because, without this selective intervention, these groups would lose out. So provision is targeted at groups and communities who, because of factors such as poverty, unemployment, ill health, and poor housing, are seen as missing out on opportunities such as education and jobs which, once they were taken up, would improve their position. This model, however, ignores the conflict of interests between groups as a result of class and other socio-economic structures of power and authority and therefore does not seek to challenge oppressive and unequal relations in our society. There is an emphasis on marginal changes which will not effect the status quo and an analysis predicated on the 'deficit' approach.

The provision that is made for women is seen, therefore, as a way of tackling 'under-achievement'. Educational interventions are designed to encourage women to 'catch-up' with men so that they can gain sufficient 'confidence' to enter into male-dominated areas. The main issue then becomes access to courses, knowledge and skills, levels of education or managerial positions not normally open to women. There is little structural analysis and the emphasis is on personal development and overcoming discriminatory practices. The purpose then of the community worker is to encourage women to successfully adapt to, rather than act on, the status quo.

This analysis leads to an acceptance of dominant social values and a strategy for change which prioritises knowledge dissemination since lack of awareness of the opportunities that are available is seen as the main cause of gender inequalities. Interventions by community workers who share this analysis are therefore based on 'starting from where people are' since, presumably, people are unable to question the world as they experience it and so opportunities which fit in with their current knowledge should be provided. Given that women are surrounded by an ideology which suggests that their primary place is as wives and mothers such an approach will do nothing to bring about social change. In a culture based on gender, as Gaskell (1992) has argued, 'Life choices come not merely from some abstract principle of what should happen, but from an assessment of the way the world works, what opportunities are open, what paths are possible'. If the only paths that are offered by community workers are those which are well-trodden and familiar then it is unlikely that there will be any challenge to the notion that the world 'as it is' is the world as it must continue to be. This means that contact is made with women through their domestic roles and caring responsibilities based on the assumption that such roles have priority over waged work and so views about women's place in the world go unchallenged.

Reflecting on the Contradictions

If community workers are going to bring about change in the material deprivations and social injustices that the state patriarchy has created for women, they need to develop a practice that promotes women's empowerment by encouraging them to articulate, understand and take action. One way in which this can be done is to help people reflect on the contradictions between their everyday lived experience of oppression and the prevailing ideology rather than just accepting the world as it is. From this position community workers would no longer implicitly espouse white, heterosexual, familialist norms about the primacy of women's domestic labour as carers of children and elders. Instead approaches could be developed which go beyond educational exit routes or recreational palliatives and provide women with opportunities to analyse their experience of waged and unwaged labour and locate their struggle as it articulates with those of other oppressed groups.

Freire (1972; 1976; 1985) has argued that, whilst it is necessary to start from people's own understanding, it is vital to do this in a 'problematising' rather than 'problem solving' way. 'Problematising' means that community workers must immerse themselves in the struggles of oppressed peoples 'through codifying total reality into symbols which can generate critical consciousness' (Freire, 1976:x) in a way which enables people to alter their social relations. This process of praxis based on critical reflection and action enables the community worker to 'tune into' the historical and cultural reality of women through developing a critical dialogue which challenges pessimistic and fatalistic thinking about how the world works.

In considering the ways in which power pervades every aspect of life it is vital to be aware that there is no such thing as political neutrality. Power, as Foucault (1977) suggests, is inscribed and manifested in our understanding of ourselves, our practices and the world. How we view ourselves and the world shapes what we view as possible and the forms of activity in which we engage. If community workers see themselves as neutrally responding to women's needs then they will, in fact, be supporting the status quo. If, at the other extreme, they espouse totalising theories that appeal to an 'essential sisterhood' then they are ignoring the differences of class, 'race' and sexuality. As Westwood (1992) points out we should 'allow among women distinctive class, racial, ethnic and sexual identities that generate similarity and difference simultaneously'. This means that community workers need to take account of the collective nature of experience within a particular locality in ways which emphasise culture, language, place, as well as class, as sources of political identification. In so doing we avoid simplistic notions of 'responding to the needs of women' through identifying: which women; in which context; and for what purpose; we are acting. As Edwards (1991) argues 'We need to problematise and politicise [our understanding] and examine ... ways in which practices and ideologies reflect/ reproduce/subvert pre-existing unequal relations of power'.

Domestication or Liberation?

There appears to be an implicit assumption that community work practice is inherently radical and liberating. However, if community workers do not examine the taken-for-grantedness of their own beliefs and values then they may end up oppressing, rather than liberating, because their unconscious assumptions and reactions reproduce the everyday practices of a socially and economically divided society. One of the most pervasive ways in which power relations operate is through myth. The myth of the community of women as carers and nurturers for whom paid work is unimportant permeates attitudes to women and work whilst the day-to-day realities of working-class women living under the shadow of this myth is of poverty, stress and hardship. Such a myth also ignores the socio-political and economic power relationships which sustain the unequal distribution of goods, services and wealth between men and women, and between women and women.

If community work practice is to become liberating rather than domesticating, then workers need to make explicit their implicit assumptions about women, class and work in ways which will enable critical reflection and action. Currently, however, most community work practice treats women as a discrete category, ignoring the complexities, conflicts and contradictions of real life. Thus, for example, it may be sufficient to use the category 'women' to describe a target group in order to access special funding. Such funding can then legitimately be used to subsidise the activities of middle class women, and many courses and groups aimed at working class women are colonised by their middle class sisters. In this way we can see how funding policies assert ideological control and enable the difficult questions posed by the realities of racism, class inequality and other oppressions to be avoided. Indeed such policies contribute to the polarisation of those who are the most oppressed and subordinated by advantaging a minority of the 'minorities'. (see Meekosha 1993).

Similarly, community work practices that either reinforce the housewifisation of women's work or fail to grapple with the cultural, political and economic shifts that are taking place, contribute to the disconnection of working-class women not only from their history, but also from a critical analysis of their relationship to the changing requirements of international capital. Much local authority community work practice falls into this domesticating arena. The curriculum – in the form of courses and activities based on a cocktail of: needs assessment; starting where people are assumed to be at; the fear of appearing too directive; and the political requirements of the employing authority – rarely engages with questions of class or the articulation of that struggle with feminism, anti-racism or other oppressed groups.

The dominant paradigm in community work rests on the principle that local communities and communities of interest, like women, have it within themselves to radically alter their material conditions. Therefore, the task of the community worker is seen as 'empowering' groups and individuals so that they can make improvements within what is tacitly assumed to be a pluralist and basically fair society. What passes for 'empowerment' under this model, however, rarely amounts to more than simply enabling groups or individuals to carry out a task, or achieve a goal, or to release their potential.

As Mayo (1994) points out, in this view empowerment is seen as 'a technique that individuals or communities can acquire in order to gain more power .... Power in society is [therefore] seen as there for the taking; you just need to learn how to do it.... If power were, in reality, equally accessible to all ... such a view would reasonably follow but, alternatively, if power is conceived in terms of its relationships with other interests in society ... then power is not there for the taking because the powerful have vested interests in defending their power'.

Conclusion

If community work practice is to be liberating, then women need to be treated as subjects of their own learning rather than objects of professional intervention (see Findlay in this volume). The emphasis needs to be on the relationship between knowledge, power and action in ways that see women's gendered experience as an educational resource to be used rather than a deficiency to be rectified. Instead of having a unitary view of the working class which is based on an outdated view of white, male, workers engaged in heavy, manual work the emphasis needs to be on the way in which class position is mediated by geographical location, sexuality, age, 'race' and gender. We need to recognise women's heterogeneity, and realise that whilst there are many sites of power there are also many sites of resistance. In these ways community workers can respect the diversity of people's lived experience but use this to promote solidarity through an understanding of oppression at both a local and a global level.

Acknowledgements

An earlier version of this article was presented at the Women's Studies Network (UK) Association annual conference on 24 June 1995.

References

Bennholdt-Thomsen, V. (1988.) The future of women's work and violence against women. *In:* M. Mies, ed. *Women – The Last Colony.* London: Zed Press

Cockburn, C. (1983). *Brothers: Male Dominance and Technological Change.* London: Pluto Press

Edwards, R. (1991). The politics of meeting learner needs: power, subject, subjection. *Studies in the Education of Adults.* 23(1) April

Engender (1994). Gender Audit, Edinburgh: Engender

Foucault, M. (1979). *The History of Sexuality, Volume 1.* London: Allen Lane

Freire, P. (1972). *Pedagogy of the Oppressed.* Harmondsworth: Penguin

Freire, P. (1976). *Education: The Practice of Freedom.* London: Writers and Readers Co-operative

Freire, P. (1985). *The Politics of Freedom.* London: Macmillan

Gaskell, J. (1992). *Gender Matters from School to Work.* Buckingham: Open University Press.

Goldthorpe, J. H. and Marshall, G. (1992). The promising future of class analysis: a response to recent critiques. *Sociology.* 26(3) August

Hart, M. (1992). *Working and Educating for Life.* London: Routledge

Hughes, M. (1993). Home base: policy on the education of women as adults. *In:* M. David, R. Edwards, M. Hughes, and J. Ribbens, eds. *Mothers and Education Inside Out?* Basingstoke: Macmillan Press.

Martin, I.S. (1993). Community education: towards a theoretical analysis. *In:* R. Edwards, E. Sieminski, and D. Zeldin, eds. *Adult Learners, Education and Training.* London: Routledge.

Mayo, M. (1994). *Communities and Caring.* Basingstoke: St Martin's Press

Meekosha, H. (1993). 'The bodies politic – equality, difference and community practice. *In:* H. Butcher, et al, eds. *Community and Public Policy.* London: Pluto Press

Oppenheim, C. (1990). *Poverty – The Facts.* London: Child Poverty Action Group

Scottish Low Pay Unit (1994) *Pay Line.* No 16, March

Sivanandan, A. (1992). Into the waste lands. *New Statesman.* 19 June

Tett, L. (1994). Where have all the men gone? *Scottish Journal of Adult and Continuing Education.* 1(2), pp41-49

United Nations (1980). UN Mid-Decade World Conference for Women, 11 – 13 July

Westwood, S. (1992). When class became community: radicalism in adult education. *In:* A. Rattansi and D. Reeder, eds. *Rethinking Radical Education.* London: Lawrence and Wishart

Chapter 9: Community Work and Lone Parents

John Findlay

Synopsis

Despite the discrimination which is experienced collectively by
lone parents, this chapter challenges the neglect of family issues in
community work. The author contends that this betrays
pathologising explanations which serve to reinforce the dominant
ideology which has demonised lone parents. Defining lone
parenthood as a 'social problem' fails to recognise the social,
political and ideological context in which this definition is
developed. Challenging community work models which locate
work on family issues within a conservative paradigm of community
care, the chapter argues for a practice which considers the
experiences of lone parents in the broader policy context,
recognising its basis in familism.

'Parochial self-interest', articulated around issues related, for
example, to after-school care can provide a basis for changing
perceptions, developing new services and reaching far beyond the
immediate neighbourhood. There is, therefore, the potential for
self-help support groups in these circumstances to provide the
focus for radical practice, linking personal experience with political
explanation and local groups with wider power structures.

Introduction

> 'I've got a little list... of young ladies who get pregnant
> just to join the housing list.' (Peter Lilley, Conservative
> Party Conference 1992)

Over the last few years family policy has been at the very centre of
political debate. Family issues have rarely been out of the headlines,
family breakdown has been blamed for a range of social ills,
delinquency, vandalism, child abuse, benefit dependency, housing

shortages – just about everything. Some politicians and academics have gone so far as to argue that lone mothers and their children are a threat to the economic and social stability of the country. Charles Murray (1994), Guru of the Right, attacks lone parents, arguing that single mothers are incapable of socialising the disruptive energy of their sons. Boys need fathers as role models, fathers who have been civilised by their wives.

'What we have taken for granted is the socialisation process because it has worked so well for so long. We have forgotten that each generation is invaded by a hoard of barbarians – our kids. Without socialisation crime is going to be astronomical and the police will have to be given more and more authority.'

This moral panic has seen the introduction of the Child Support Act, (1991) amendment of the Homeless Persons legislation, the Back to Basics fiasco and the creation of a climate of fear and apprehension amongst lone parents. The implementation of punitive legislation is justified on the premise that one parent families are a social problem requiring a public policy response.

Family issues – personal and political

For most lone parents the process of becoming a lone parent signals a sharp fall in living standards – reduced income, poorer housing, unemployment and so on, all flowing from their changed family circumstances. One-parent families are thus, a marginalised group experiencing a level of discrimination and stereotyping which is used to justify a range of punitive legislation. On the face of it, therefore, family issues are a legitimate area for community work involvement. However, this is an area of practice which has often been neglected. In this chapter I will argue that we should be working in this area and attempt to identify the underlying reasons for this neglect. I will then consider the potential of working with lone parents and, in particular, highlight the impact local action can have on the wider political agenda.

Traditionally, lone parents have been defined as 'problem families' requiring support on an individualised basis within a social work context. Group work has been viewed in terms of developing self-help groups which provide mutual support rather than organising around issues of common concern aimed at affecting social change. Many community workers have argued that work of this kind with lone parents is stigmatising, confirms stereotypes and is therefore not a basis for collective action. To work in such a way, they argue, would be to confirm Waddington's (1983) analysis that the community work task could become:

> 'To manage the multiplicity of new groups and organisations which will be brought into being to engage the long term structurally unemployed and to provide the new community based social services.'

Change, in this account, is localised, specific to certain areas of activity and aimed at helping people cope with their situation rather than challenge it. In short, work with lone parents to help organise mutual self-help groups is a social work issue and therefore not an issue for community work involvement.

However, an analysis of the position of lone parents highlights the importance of family issues on both the political and personal level. Why is it that lone parents are regarded as such a threat to society? Why have they been marginalised, stigmatised and scapegoated? The demonisation of single parents is used to justify the implementation of oppressive legislation on the basis that they are not the 'deserving' poor. For example, in all the controversy surrounding the implementation of the Child Support Act, the fact that it contains the harshest benefit penalty in the D.S.S. armoury has hardly merited a mention. Similarly, the change in the homelessness legislation in England was justified by juxtaposing the nice young couple unable to obtain a house with the feckless teenage single parent who gets pregnant simply to jump the housing queue. These are all seen as perfectly acceptable propositions because 'lone parents do not deserve any better'.

At a more fundamental level, Murray's (1994) work provides a spurious theoretical basis for this type of legislation. He argues that, by withdrawing benefits, people will be forced to bear the consequences of their behaviour:

> 'Gradually a traditional morality will re-emerge – society's natural way or organising itself – whereby the

two parent family becomes the norm again and bastards and single mothers are stigmatised.'

To understand why Murray and his followers believe the nuclear two parent family is so important a critical analysis of the role of the family is required. What is offered is, of course, an ideology which promotes two parent families as an ideal type but which bears little or no resemblance to the reality of the family and all its forms. The nuclear family, which he presents as a natural phenomenon, is in fact a product of the late eighteenth century and is bound up in the relationship between patriarchy and the development of industrial capitalist society. Since the family is a social construct, there is no clear unambiguous definition of what a family is and, indeed, the nature of the family changes from culture to culture. Families are highly complex and fluid social groupings. By definition, therefore, families are constantly changing. The promotion therefore of an ideal family type represents for Gittins (1988):

'An historical class specific ideology premised on earlier partriarchical religious ideals and beliefs. This ideology does not represent the reality of how individuals interact together. Yet it manifests just enough similarity to people's life situation as to make it seem tangible and real to most. Thus the never married, the divorced and the childless can at least identify part of the 'ideal family' with a past childhood or family distorted in memory and feel that their own 'failure' has been an individual failing rather than an unrealistic ideal'.

The strength of this hegemony can be seen from the impact on family policy. The current benefits system grew from the principles outlined in the Beveridge Report (1944), in which the family consisted of men as bread winners and women as housewives and child carers.

'The attitude of the housewife to gainful employment outwith the house is not and should not be the same as that of a single woman she has other duties.'

Whilst the sociological landscape has changed considerably since the Beveridge Report, there is still a considerable investment in promoting the nuclear family as the foundation of a healthy society with men in the role of provider and women in the role of mother caring for children, both required as role models for children as they grow up.

'Real' and 'pretend' families

However, as highlighted earlier, a tension exists between the ideology which promotes the ideal type nuclear family and the reality of family life. More is expected of marriage than in the past with greater emphasis on the romantic and compassionate ideal:

> 'Where not long ago marriage was presented as a working partnership with the husband the acknowledged head the primary purpose of which was to produce children it has been presented increasingly as a loving relationship between two equal partners whose aim is to create domestic harmony through co-operation, mutual sexual gratification and the careful and loving rearing of two or three children. As an ideal and one which has to survive a long test of time this is a tall order and one that is unlikely to survive in reality for long.' (Gittens, 1988)

Furthermore, the demographics of family life also demonstrate that the truth is very different from the image. The numbers of families headed by a lone parent is growing in all the western industrial societies.

Table 1

Country	Percentage	Year	
Britain	*21	1990	This was put together from a variety of sources: Denmark, France, Sweden – Un parent seul dans une famille sur huit; INSEE 1994; Germany, Italy, Luxembourg, Portugal – 12 Wege der Familienpolitik in der EG BMFUS 1993; Britain – General Household Survey 1992;139 OPCS 1994. There are no figures at all for Greece and figures from Belgium, Ireland and Spain date from 1980-81 and were compiled on a different basis.
Denmark	22	1990	
France	12	1990	
Germany	17	1989	
Italy	6	1989	
Luxembourg	7	1989	
Netherlands	18	1988	
Portugal	6	1990	
Sweden	22	1990	

*all children under 16 and those under 18 still in full-time education.

At a local level in Strathclyde the numbers of lone parents has increased from 44,673 in 1981 to 68,090 in 1991 – an increase from 14.6% to 24.3% of all families with children. The vast majority of lone parent families are formed as a result of relationship breakdown as follows:

Table 2: OPCS, Population Trends No 71, 1991 Census.

Family Type	Percentage of Total	Numbers:
Separated	19	235,000
Divorced	34	415,000
*Single	32	390,000
Men	9	110,000
Widows	6	75,000

*Many of these will be women who have lived with their partners but are now separated (55% of all births outside marriage are registered by both parents who live at the same address).

Much of the media coverage has concentrated on the number of women who are not married, asserting that this number is rising as a percentage of all lone parents. However, what is not mentioned is the fact that the majority of live births outside marriage were registered by both parents. In 1991, for example, 74.4% of live births outside marriage in Britain were registered by both parents and 54.6% were registered by both parents at the same address. In other words to be unmarried does not necessarily mean to be on your own. Nor does it indicate a denial of family committment. It does, however, suggest that the necessity of marriage to this commitment is under question.

Another aspect of the 'family in crisis' debate has been the myth that the number of teenage mothers has been rising. The truth is that the number of teenage mothers has actually fallen substantially from the peak reached in the period 1965 – 1969. In 1992 there were 5,203 births to women under 20 years of age compared with an average of 9,000 in the period 1965 – 1974. What has risen is the proportion of those under 20 years of age who are not married. Births to unmarried mothers as a percentage of all births to under 20s has risen from 18.7% in 1949 to 85% in 1992 (Registrar General Scotland, 1992).

To a large extent, therefore, the growing numbers of lone parents can be seen as a consequence of the failure of the nuclear family as the ideal type. To acknowledge this publicly, however, would be to call into question the whole basis of 'the family'; it is more convenient to promote the myth of the young feckless single parent.

> 'Family ideology has been a vital means of holding together and legitimising the existing social, economic, political and gender systems. Challenging the ideology this means challenging the whole social system.'(Gittens, 1988)

If we accept this analysis then the need to vilify, scapegoat and marginalise lone parents becomes clear

The reality of lone parenthood

The ideology of the nuclear family not only underpins our current benefit system but all aspects of social policy – the education system, employment patterns, access to childcare and so on. The impact of family policy across the board, therefore, means that lone parents face a range of inter-related issues trapping them in poverty. These are:

- access to flexible affordable high quality childcare
- access to education/training
- poverty benefits/low pay
- housing
- isolation.

None of these factors operate in isolation but interact with each other. Lack of access to childcare – the U.K. has one of the poorest levels of provision in Europe – means that lone parents have to pay for childcare. To be able to afford to pay for childcare and escape the regressive nature of the benefits system requires well paid employment which requires a high level of training which requires access to affordable childcare – a vicious circle. Low income also means that housing choices are constrained, often resulting in dependence on public housing stock which is distant from family/friend support networks requiring access to childcare, without which they are trapped in the isolation of the home. In this way the experience of lone parents is individualised.

The net result of this combination of circumstances is that 75% of lone parents depend on Income Support. In Scotland 80% of lone parents are dependent on their local authority for housing. In Strathclyde this means that lone parent families are concentrated in areas of high unemployment and poor housing – Areas of Priority Treatment (A.P.T.). 42% of all lone parent households live in APTs compared to 26% of all households (S.R.C. 1992). In 1992 one parent families made up 40% of all homeless lets in Glasgow (Glasgow City Council). In the last 10 years the employment rates of lone mothers has fallen whilst the employment rates of mothers with partners has been rising.

Country	Percentage	Year
Britain *21	1990	
Denmark	22.00	1990

In 1992 the gross weekly disposable income of a one parent family was only 38.2% that of a two parent family (General Statistics Office, 1992). Nearly 50% of all children received into care live in a one parent family (SRC, 1991). These are damning statistics which highlight the failure of family policy – not of individual lone parents.

One parent families, whilst they face a number of problems in trying to escape the poverty trap should not be defined as 'problem families' which individualises what are essentially structural problems. In the light of this I would argue that the status of being a lone parent is a basis for bringing people together to challenge the dominant ideology of the nuclear family and the oppressive legislation based upon it. Collective action on this basis is no more stigmatising than black people coming together to challenge racism. It is an important issue and one which community workers should not ignore. For me the central question is how we bring lone parents together, not whether we should.

The straitjacket of community work theory

As highlighted earlier family issues and, in particular, issues of lone parents have not been the focus of a great deal of community work activity. I believe that part of the problem in addressing this issue has been the theoretical strait-jacket in which community work has operated, whereby particular practices and approaches have been uncritically located in and linked with certain ideological positions (see Barr, 1982):

Location of problem:

* individualistic
* governmental
* structural

Expressed politically as:

* Conservative
* Reformist
* Radical

And in community work terms as:

* community care
* community development
* community action.

By doing this we imbue the terms community care, community action and community development with assumed ideological stances. The impact of these assumptions on community work has been to define certain activities e.g. community care, as informed by conservative ideology, obscuring the underlying issues which need to be addressed. Identifying community care as individualistic stems from a social pathology explanation of the problem and behavioural change as the solution (see Shaw in this volume). By virtue of their definition as social problems, lone parents are located in the same 'care' paradigm.

I believe that this has been a positive block to the development of community work with lone parents. The stereotypical view of the lone parent family as dysfunctional, requiring social work support has led to work with lone parents being seen as a therapeutic process rather than as a community work issue. We need to free the activity or, more appropriately, the label attached to it from its ideological connotations. Work with lone parents can be regressive and encourage dependence if it starts from this stereotypical view. It can, alternatively however, recognise the collective oppression experienced by lone parents and work towards bringing people together to challenge hegemonic definitions.

Personal troubles into public issues

Once the prevailing view that work with lone parents is a social work issue is challenged and seen to be flawed, then the potential of community work can begin to be developed. The starting point has to take into account the current position of most lone parents – the fact that 75% are trapped in poverty, together with the negative stereotyping which compounds their marginalisation. We need to engage with the reality of living in poverty, in bad housing, with little prospect of employment, and little or no access to childcare.

In such circumstances, simply surviving requires enormous energy, let alone becoming involved in campaigning. The mental and physical efforts of living in poverty are well documented and include depression, drug/alcohol dependency, low life expectancy, apathy, exhaustion. Compounding this are the constant attacks in the media and a hostile political environment. It is not surprising, therefore, that community workers experience difficulties in encouraging lone parents to organise around issues of family policy and national legislation. Lone parents feel powerless in their ability to have an impact on government legislation in the current ideological climate.

In view of this, lone parents often have to develop sufficient confidence to tackle the issues facing them. Community workers are well-placed to offer educational support. If this stage is missed then the danger is that we will simply continue to work with those community groups which attract the most confident, experienced activists – often those with experience of the formal labour and trade union movement. At its worse, this approach can create community hierarchies which mimic to a large extent the structures of the local authority and state bureaucracies they were established to challenge.

Working with lone parents, therefore, may in the first instance require developing a short term strategy; for example, self-help groups to provide mutual support to lone parents. Such support groups are often ignored by community workers due, precisely, to the connotations of the community care typology outlined earlier. However, by engaging with this type of group a starting point can be established to build confidence, share problems and assert the collective nature of the experience – redefining the problem as the failure of family policy, not personal failure. Issues can then be identified and relevant responses developed. These issues can be many and varied – lack of childcare, bad housing, the length of the school day, post office closure, baby clinic facilities and so on. Lone parent groups have, in fact, been the main force behind many out of school care schemes, mobile crèches and sitter services which have obtained urban aid funding and attracted European Social Fund grants. However, for Barr (1991) there is a danger that community organisations formed in this way concentrate solely on parochial interests:

> 'while they may recognise a wider aggregate interest at city wide or even national level neighbourhood residents quite rationally assess the potential for change on the evidence that is available that local pressure and redirecting existing resources is easier to achieve than any overall increase.'

Waddington (1983), from a different stance, comes to similar conclusions, warning that community action on a localised basis could be seen as 'mindless activism'.

> 'In the 70's successful localised community action campaigns fed off the annual surplus of a growing economy and were part of a system of public sector redistribution to disadvantaged and marginal groups. This provided the baits which were the initial stimulus for community action. In a shrinking public sector many community work activities as originally conceived have simply lost their point.'

For Barr this means that community work needs to adopt a social policy role linked into overall assessments based on equity and social justice. For Waddington, community workers would have to seek out 'these aspects of their work which left space of any kind for a radical input'.

What emerges from this debate is that neighbourhood work seems to have a very limited potential. However, I believe that both these positions fail to recognise the potential of locally based campaigns, both in terms of the establishment of new forms of service delivery and impact on the national political agenda. Moreover, to do so does not necessarily require the establishment of large scale federated organisations which are a reflection of the labour and trade union movement.

After-school care as a basis for action

The development of after-school care is a useful case study which highlights the potential of work with lone parents and the wider impact this can have. Fifteen years ago there were few, if any, after-school care services operating in Strathclyde. In fact, it was not seen as an issue in childcare, equal opportunity or economic development terms. However, childcare is an important issue for women and in, particular, lone parents. In 1980 a group of lone parents in a Glasgow housing estate had come together on a self-help basis and from this identified the common need to access childcare and, in particular, care for their school age children. The group decided to campaign for resources to establish an after-school care scheme. This involved meeting, discussing with and persuading the education and social work departments, the local authority and the Scottish Office that the service was both important and viable. However, the need for after-school care was met with fairly widespread scepticism and, in some cases, outright hostility; but the argument was won and the first Urban-Aided after school service in Strathclyde was established.

Once this was achieved the project decided to work to support the development of after-school care schemes in other areas. From this, after-school care was established in the surrounding areas and then in other parts of Strathclyde. In 1984 it was established that there was a need for a federated organisation and Strathclyde After-School Care Association (SASCA) was established. In 1987, after a protracted campaign to establish the need for an umbrella organisation, SASCA received urban aid funding and, once established, the rate of progress increased. Other parts of Scotland began to develop similar structures, with Lothian Region establishing ALASCA to carry out similar functions to SASCA. It was then a short step to recognising the need for a national body, and in 1993 the Scottish Out of School Network was established.

In the space of 15 years a national network has been established and after-school care has been widely recognised as an important childcare, equal opportunity and economic development issue. The government has also acknowleded the importance of school age childcare, albeit inadequately, by developing the Childcare Initiative which is administered by the Local Enterprise Companies (LECs). Whilst not wishing to over-estimate this impact, the development of after-school care has, to a large extent, been led by local community organisations. A new area of childcare practice has been identified and developed at a local level, supported in many cases by community workers. It is doubtful that a social planning approach would necessarily have identified this issue. Indeed, the development of after-school care highlights the power of 'parochial interest' (i.e. the need for childcare) to change perceptions, develop new services and reach far beyond the immediate neighbourhood. Those who have been involved in this process have, to some extent, been empowered, by linking local issues with wider potential power structures and developing federated organisations.

I have focused particularly on the example of the development of after-school care, as the establishment of affordable childcare is a key issue for lone parents wishing to return to work, take part in education, attend community groups and improve their quality of life. By developing and organising for improved childcare facilities, the ideology of the idealised nuclear family is being challenged and the validity of all family types endorsed.

Conclusion

In this chapter I have argued that the position of lone parents is created by the failure of family policy which, in itself, is built on the ideology of the idealised nuclear family. Lone parents are attacked for not conforming to this ideal type and are severely disadvantaged by legislation designed to promote the nuclear family. The range of discrimination faced by lone parents means that this is a legitimate area of community work activity – sometimes neglected because, in its early stages, the process has been viewed as conforming to a community care model. I have argued that this model has been inappropriately linked to a certain ideological stance which has limited the development of community work practice. In developing work with lone parents it is sometimes appropriate in the first instance, to work with self-help groups, through which participants build their confidence and collectively identify issues of concern.

I focused on the development of after-school care to highlight the potential impact local groups can have on the national agenda, which in this case, challenges current family policy and the ideology which underpins it. Community work has played an important role in this process and retains its validity in assisting people to come together on issues of collective concern which challenge current orthodoxies at both a local and national level.

References

Un Parent Seul Dans Une Famille Sur Huit (1994) INSEE

Social Trends (1992) Strathclyde Regional Council

Families in the Future – A Policy Agenda for the 80's, Study Commission on the Family Social Policy Section (1983) Glasgow City Council

CENSUS Population Trends No. 71 (1991) HMSO

General Household Survey (1992) Office of Population Censuses and Surveys

Family Expenditure Survey (1992) HMSO General Statistics Office

Annual Report of Registrar General Scotland (1992) General Registrar for Scotland

Social Work Department (1991) Strathclyde Regional Council

The Family Fact File – Family Policy Studies Centre 16 Incorporating Family Forum (1991) Family Policy Studies Centre 16

DSS Annual Statistical Enquiry (1990) HMSO

Barr A. (1982). Practice Models and Training Issues in Bidwell and McConnell Eds. *Community Education and Community Development*. Dundee College of Education

Barr A. (1991). *Practising Community Development*. Community Development Foundation

Beveridge. (1944) Beveridge Report

Brannen J. and Moss P. (1988). *New Mothers At Work – Employment and Childcare*. Unwin

Cousins J. and Coote A. (1984). *The Family In The Firing Line*. NCCL and CPAG

Dames S. (1989). *A Decade of Damage Done To Families*. Social Work Today

Deakin N. and Wicks M. (1988). *Families and The State*. Family Policies Study Centre

Dumon W. (1992). National Family Policies in EC Countries in 1991. Volume 1. Directory General for Employment

Edgerton J. (1991). *The Family Way*. Trouble and Strife

Fletcher R. (1988). *The Shaking Of The Foundations Family and Society*. Routledge

Gittins D. (1988). *The Family in Question Changing Households and Familiar Ideologies*. MacMillan Education

Kiernan K. and Wicks M. (1990) *Family Change and Future Policy*. Joseph Rowntree Memorial Trust and Family Policy Studies Centre

Laurer J.C. and Laurer R.H. (1986). *Till Death Do us Part*. Harrington Park Press

Murray C. (1994). The Guardian 17.9.94

Rapaport R.N., Fogarty M.P. and Rapaport R. (1982). *Families In Britain*. Routledge

Roll J. (1991). *What Is A Family? Benefit Models and Social Realities*. Family Policy Studies Centre

Waddington P. (1983). *Looking Ahead* in D.N. Thomas Ed *Community Work In The Eighties*. National Institute for Social Work

Wicks M. and Harman H. (1991). The Family Vote, *Community Care* 10.1.91

Chapter 10: Anti-Racist Community Work – A Radical Approach

Rowena Arshad

Synopsis

In this chapter, the author develops the basis of a radical agenda in the fight against racism in Scotland. She develops an analysis which rejects the dichotomies of race and culture in an attempt to understand and address the causes and processes of racism. The distinction between respect for cultural difference and the 'culturing of politics' is used to reassert the need to understand and engage with the complexities of identity within a politics of solidarity. Focussing on the work of a project which has brought together both black and white communites to support a campaign for a Nigerian family threatened by immigration laws, she draws out a framework for practice which moves beyond mere rhetoric or sloganising.

Introduction

When considering my contribution to a book about Radical community work, in relation to anti-racist work, I had to first ask whether there has ever been a radical agenda in the fight against racism in Scotland. Indeed, what might a radical agenda look like?

Up until the mid 1980s, what tended to predominate in Scottish political discourse was a sense that Scotland had 'good race relations' and that there was 'no problem' here (see Miles and Dunlop 1986; Dunlop 1993). Consequently, racism did not become an issue within Scottish political or policy debates. Since the mid-1980s, however, Scottish thinking has, in general, shifted from a stance of total complacency to one that accepts, be it grudgingly , that racism is not a problem confined to areas of high black populations such as Birmingham or Tower Hamlets (see Arshad and McCrum, 1989). Professionals both Black[1] and white began campaigning for policies

---

1. I have chosen to used the word 'Black' in this chapter with a capital to denote that it is used as a political term to include people who suffer racism under white-

and practices that would effect changes in life-chances for Black people in Scotland. These initiatives and efforts were undertaken within a discourse of 'anti-discriminatory practice', 'multicultural and anti-racist education', 'race equality action', 'equal opportunities' and 'positive action'.

However, characteristics which distinguish radical anti-racist community work remain ambiguous. This chapter attempts to define such a model with the reminder that models are not blue-prints but abstractions. As Martin (1987) states 'such 'ideal-types' are exploratory rather than definitive, analytical rather descriptive'. Before attempting to construct such a model, it is necessary to identify some of the issues surrounding the debate about 'race'[2] equality work with which community workers have had to explore and grapple.

Multicultural or anti-racist approaches?

The debate about multicultural versus anti-racist approaches originated in the early 1980s (see Sivanandan, 1985; Hatcher, 1987; Brown and Lawton, 1991; Klein, 1993). Multicultural approaches were criticised for focussing exclusively on cultures; of being preoccupied with exotic aspects of cultural difference thereby ignoring the effects of racism. Moreover, opponents of multicultural approaches (see Mullard 1982; Sarup, 1991) argued that they assumed people started from an equal base when that was clearly not so. Racial discrimination and injustice were pervasive in British society. Much has been documented about how this has affected the livelihoods and life chances of Black people in key areas like education and employment (see Troyna, 1987; Haynes, 1983).

In this context, anti-racism and anti-racist approaches were seen as alternatives to multiculturalism in that they embraced an analysis of the issues of power and justice arguing for basic changes in the power structures of society. Sociologists like Sarup (1991) advocated that anti-racism 'includes multicultural education, and goes beyond it.'

dominated structures. It represents people who share a common experience, it is a political category rather like one uses the word 'red' or 'green'.

2. The term 'race' is included within quote marks in recognition that this term is problematic. As it bears no scientific validity, it is an ideology. However the common sense and ideological notion has effects and is enshrined within law as in the Race Relations Act. As a recognition of this point, the reader is asked bear this in mind when reading the word race in this chapter

The debate of multicultural versus anti-racist approaches is still on going. Klein (1993) states, however, that the debate is perhaps not as polarised as presented. Many educationalists (including community workers) who take into account issues of power, equality and justice are also keen supporters of cultural exchanges and cultural programmes such as multicultural drama festivals, multicultural story telling sessions, multicultural book fairs and so on. To suggest that multiculturalists were not anti-racists in these instances would neither be accurate nor fair. To suggest that anti-racists were not supportive of cultural events and exchanges would be equally mis-representative.

The issue for community workers intent on a radical agenda might, therefore, not be so much which approach is adopted but rather how to develop an understanding of the causes and processes of racism. Whilst it is important to be able to quote statistics of racist incidents and to point to the effects of racism as evidenced by the extent of racial disadvantage, it is equally important to be able to identify how it is operating as an effective force in the life of the communities we work within today. This understanding can come about by working with and talking to Black people and by conceptualising an analysis of racism that does not deny the structural aspects of racism in Scottish society and within Scottish institutions.

By extension, radical community work would therefore assist people (both Black and white) to organise and respond to institutionalised racism (see Wester Hailes Against Racism Project later in this chapter). It would support activities which affect the lives of those oppressed by racist structures; it would get involved in issues of immigration, illegal deportations and campaigns against racial harassment. It would encompass, but move beyond, the realms of personal prejudices. Failure to engage with the processes and dynamics of racism, from its roots in the 17th century to its manifestations as we approach the millennium, will lead to continued confusion about strategies which might be adopted to ensure radical social change.

Let us explore, for example, a situation where structural power was utilised in a subtle manner to generate confused policies and practice and which, in fact, resulted in a perpetuation of institutionalised racism. Although this situation occurred within a discourse of race equality, the old assimilationist paradigm was subtly adapted and added to instead of being redefined:

In the wake of discontent in Brixton, Southall, Liverpool, Manchester and throughout at least 27 other towns in England in

1981, the Government commissioned the Scarman Report (quoted in Sivanandan, 1983). In Scarman, the uprisings were attributed to the 'ill-considered, immature and racially prejudiced actions of some officers in their dealings on the street with young people' (Scarman 1982). The problem was, therefore, defined as prejudice which manifested itself occasionally in the behaviour of a few, unthinking ignorant and isolated individuals. In this account, individual errors can be punished and ignorant individuals can be assisted to rationality by undergoing *attitudinal change*. This is an essentially liberal perspective in which issues of differentials in power between the police and young people and between white and Black remained unaddressed.

In 1985, the Swann Report was published – the outcome of the deliberations of the Rampton Committee which was set up to deal with the problems of Black children. Its primary focus was the growing underachievement of African and Caribbean children in mainstream education. Racism, as a contributory cause of underachievement, was identified but the Report was indecisive in its advice as to which model of practice would best eliminate either racism or underachievement. Issues relating to control of the curriculum, the conduct of educational assessments, and who set the tests were side-stepped in favour of a focus on 'cultural tolerance'. In focussing on the children and their disadvantage, instead of the racism which the Report itself identified as a contributory cause to the underachievement, the real issues remain unresolved. These problems and disadvantages were associated with cultural and linguistic characteristics of the 'immigrants' themselves – problems which they brought with them. The perceived role of 'immigrant' language and customs as a cause of disadvantage and an obstacle to assimilation saw the Labour Government in the mid 1960s release monies under the infamous Section 11 to the Education Departments within Authorities to ensure that these disadvantages could be reduced by:

> '... providing smaller classes in which English can be adequately taught, as well as providing extra visitors to remind parents of their new obligations in Britain, it is essential to teach these children basic British customs, basic British habits and, if one likes, basic British prejudices – all those things which they need to know if

they are to live happily and successfully in an integrated
way in this community'. [Hansard 1966, col 1336]

Both these reports formed the basis of many of the Equal
Opportunity initiatives within Scottish Local Authorities and the
projects they supported within the voluntary sector. My purpose in
highlighting these two reports is not to engage in invidious
comparisons, but to draw upon two key tenets which have proven to
be vanguards of racism. The first has been to contain the challenge
against racism to a personal level, and the second has been to engage
in offering token and short-term projects for black people rather than
working to dismantle the system that perpetuates racial oppression.
In this way, the faceless forces of racism continue to operate, obtaining
legitimation from the silent and often uninformed majority. The
essential point of both reports was the pathologisation of racism.

Radical anti-racist community work practice, then, needs to
recognise that pathological explanations are not ambiguous and, if
we aim to enhance the life-chances of those suffering racism, we
cannot afford to be ambiguous.

In search of difference – beyond anti-racism?

'The 'assertion of difference' has become, for many radicals, the
principal dynamic in society today' (Malik, 1996). Stuart Hall, a
leading Black sociologist, has welcomed the flowering of different
ethnicities as an expression, not of social discord, but a new form of
democracy through which the voices of the many previously silenced
could now be heard.

The idea that all groups have a right to speak for themselves, in
their own voice; and to have that voice accepted as authentic and
legitimate is an attractive proposition for many who work with people
and communities who have been marginalised, and excluded.
Community workers, committed to social justice and anti-
discrimination, may well be attracted to an approach which, on the
surface, appears to encourage the expression of individual identities.

The last decade has witnessed an increased desire particularly
from the white communities to learn about different cultures and
lifestyles. The hope was that such knowledge would bring about better
race relations and eradicate racial discrimination. Educational
programmes began to offer sessions where pupils and public alike
could learn about 'a taste of India' or 'family life in a Traveller

community in Ireland' for example. Libraries stocked up on books about different lifestyles so that we coud learn about how different cultures cared for *their* elderly, conducted *their* marriage rites, and cooked *their* exciting cuisines.

In this sense, a 'culturing of politics' has occurred. The notion of 'society' is reduced to the aggregate of individual relationships and the 'social', nothing more than a particular decision that any individual may make (Malik, 1996). Indeed, trying to understand multiple social identities has led to anxieties that there are conflicting social pressures and identities. Given that cultures are not static or stable, is it ever possible to comprehend all these subjectivities? If no two experiences or cognitions are identical, because of the way identities depend minutely on the contexts in which they appear, how then can the practitioner work with communities in an appropriate and truly culturally sensitive manner?

Radical anti-racist community work would encompass the need to understand the complexity of identity politics , to recognise there can be different subjectivities and to grasp that everyone juggles different identities for the sake of expediency, or to enjoy the position of 'belonging'. None of these identities are to be trivialised, but seen to derive from a person's experience – their interpretation of the various knowledges and discourses they have been exposed to. However, a conceptualising of this as multiple and dynamic must be done both within a politics of solidarity and an analysis of the causes and effects of structural discrimination. Indeed, failure to do so can leave the practitioner hostage to the prejudices and whims of particular groups or individuals they are working with at any given time.

Within a radical anti-racist model, fundamental social relations such as racism and racial oppression do not become reduced to lifestyle choices. A radical approach would make connections with other forms of disadvantage and discrimination (see Shaw, Petrie and Cooke in this volume). The comments of Sivanandan (1995), Director of the Institute of Race Relations is helpful when he urges us to:

> '... organise not for culture but against racism, against fascism, against the erosion of civil liberties, against injustice and inequality – against racism *qua* racism instead of particularising the racisms. We are organising not for the Bangladeshis (in the East End of London) but against racism ...'

We need also to be aware of how the New Right have hijacked the debate about identity and difference. Their acknowledgement of difference, of course, is not with the intended outcome of equalising differences but to assist categorisation – to promote an implicit xenophobic message that 'difference' equals 'deficit'.

Terminology and political correctness

There has been much debate during the last few years about terminology. Challenging racist language has laid the anti-racist movement open to accusations of attempting to be the thought police, curtailing free speech and denying 'common sense'. Words like 'black', which were once used by black activists and supporters of the Civil Rights Movement in the United States during the 1960s to reclaim and re-establish Black identity, became linked in the 1990s to an hysteria against political correctness. Virulent campaigns by the tabloid press about 'loony left' councils who sacked childminders for having golliwogs or who banned the singing of 'Baa Baa, Black Sheep' in schools, resulted in anti-racist terminology offending the Right and confusing the Left. For the Right, this has been in character with their ideological purpose of denying voice to different social movements and groups thereby denying them a right to be participants within political struggle and discourse. The attempt to debunk 'Black' as a political category is part of that process.

However, the confusion of the Left on anti-racism and political correctness is an altogether more tragic affair in that the fear of challenging racist language has also led to a fear of challenging the assumptions built into our ordinary use of language and its implications. Struggles over language are not necessarily over the terms themselves, but, rather, their connotative meaning (e.g. the Black is Beautiful slogan sought to ascribe positive meaning). Such confusion also obscures the distinction between the coupling of terms in a logical way and those coupled ideologically. For example, it would be logical to use a term like blackboard if the board was black; whereas terms like 'blacklist' and 'blackmark' have connotations which are negative.

If one of the key aspects of radical community work practice is to challenge racism and reclaim lost history – the history of Black people over the centuries – then this has to include an analysis of how language has been used to demean different ethnic groupings. There are many historical examples where the conduct of a social struggle has depended on the dis-articulation of terms which have been previously used to further oppress or marginalise. Feminism's challenge to the overall usage of terms like 'he' to encompass both male and female, is one such example.

Within this chapter, I have used the term 'black' as a political term, to define any individual or group who suffers racism because of their skin colour. This perspective by no means negates the diversity of Black people, nor does it deny that discrimination exists against other groups, who may or may not have defined themselves as 'ethnic minorities', such as travellers or Irish people. Understanding the political meaning of the term 'black' is, however, a necessary step for constructing an anti-racist agenda. To understand 'black' in its political context is to site it squarely within the structural manifestations of racism, thereby removing the debate from a personal, individualised one, to one which recognises the 'superstructure' – how colour, as a category, has been used to differentiate people into high and low status groups for discriminatory purposes.

Raising the issue of racism causes the problem!

It is no easy task to balance the right of the individual within the context of the common good. Sandel (1994: 54) an American professor of government argues that 'intolerance actually flourishes where life is dislocated, roots unsettled and traditions undone.' Sceptics of anti-racism have often used such thinking to prevent work that would allow people to engage in critical thinking within the area of multiculturalism and anti-racism, on the basis that it would breed a backlash. The logic of Sandel's argument, within a Scottish context, is that Scots, being predominantly white, may feel *naturally* unaccustomed or threatened by other cultures and ethnic groupings. To enforce a programme of anti-racist initiatives may, therefore, be to impose irrelevancy to people's real life experiences, thereby causing discordance and disharmony where none previously existed. Resistance to anti-racist work is often prefaced by statements like: 'there are no black people here', 'the real issue here is ...' or 'why bring it up and make it an issue, when it is not one...'.

This fear of backlash, and the prospect of even more reactionary consequences, have held some workers back from being pro-active against racism or have channelled their energies into other forms of generalised discrimination such as anti-poverty work, or work around issues such as homelessness or drugs, whilst often, in the process, side-stepping anti-racist work.

Radical community work, with its premise firmly located within an analysis of power and structural inequality should surely seek to encompass the challenge against racism, recognising that failure to make connections across issues is likely to leave racism unacknowledged and unchallenged. Ohri et al writing in the early 1980s stressed that there are two objective facts which community workers need to accept and internalise in order to address the issue of racism. The first is that Britain is a multi-racial society; the second, that racism has infected 'the consciousness' of both individuals and institutions in this society.

A radical community work practice would seek to expose the way in which racism has infected this consciousness – both personally and structurally. It would seek to work with people in ways that would challenge dominant Eurocentric values, organising to ensure that both black and white would begin dialogues to construct a new paradigm.

Building fragile bridges

A lesson, unambiguously learnt from the MacDonald Inquiry in 1989 which investigated the murder of thirteen year old Asian pupil, Ahmed Ullah, by a white boy Darren Colbourn (also 13), in Manchester, was the need to make connections between different forms of oppression. Ahmed was a victim of racism, Darren was a victim of class oppression. The school's anti-racist approaches were confined to working with Black pupils and parents. White parents and pupils were not included in these initiatives, thereby relegating them to the role of 'baddies'. Two lessons emerged from Burnage; firstly, the struggle against racism needs equally, to be a struggle against other forms of inequality and, secondly, as racism damages all of us, then everyone, both Black and white, has to be brought into the fight against racism. It is not the responsibility of one group alone.

Radical anti-racist community work demands a politics of solidarity, linking experiences and identifying core elements of similarities between groups as the beginning of the sustenance of an agenda for radical change. Hilary Wainwright (1991) argues that social movements, whilst successful in releasing and expressing everyday knowledge, have been less so in the coordination of such knowledge. As community workers, we have been fairly successful in creating space for people to come together to develop and to engage in self-help – for example, women's groups and girls' work – but we have been less strategic in achieving a coordination of such spaces to ensure the emergence of a radical anti-discriminatory project. How does girls work link to work with boys; how does feminist thinking link to work with men (see Meagher and Tett in this volume)?. How should feminists work with men? These discourses are yet to be opened up within the community work agenda. Similarly, if black and white are to work together, then community workers need to assist in organising for these energies and concerns to come together.

Community work practice: from dialogue to action

So far, I have explored some issues surrounding race work, which community workers have had to grapple with at both conceptual and practical levels. How can this move beyond the rhetoric? The following case-study is shared as an example of innovative practice. An evaluation of the implications for radical anti-racist community work practice and development are summarised at the end.

Wester Hailes Against Racism Project (WHARP) and the Adegboye Family Support Campaign – A case study.
WHARP has just completed its first year of operation. It has a small multi-racial staff team of four workers (two full-time, one part-time and one administrator). WHARP's main aim is to identify the needs of the black/minority ethnic communities in Wester Hailes and to work to promote their rights, aspirations and entitlements. WHARP received Urban Programme funding and is supported by the local authority community education service. The need for a project like WHARP was identified by local agencies and the Community Education Service. Consultation with locals, Black or white about the ethos and aims of WHARP, prior to its commencement, appear to have been minimal or nonexistent.

WHARP staff identified the need, from the outset, to establish credibility with local black/minority ethnic residents. Did local people really want a Project like WHARP? If so, how could the Project best meet their needs? To find out, I interviewed the Project Coordinator, Andy Egan.

Q: *How did WHARP begin work in Wester Hailes?*

Andy: *WHARP is a Black community development project. At the start of the Project,we knew we needed to make contact with Black/minority ethnic residents and to build up credibility. We needed to identify the needs of local people based on their experiences of racism. We carried out a structural needs survey which actually covered specific forms of racism such as racial harassments, immigration and nationality issues as well as general areas such as housing, employment and education.*

Q: *Why did you include immigration and nationality as categories in the survey?*

Andy: *Because of our awareness as a staff team that these issues were central to the experiences of a significant number of black/ minority ethnic people. These areas were also included as important after much consultation with other agencies with experience in this area of work*

Q: *How did you go about conducting the survey?*

Andy: *We had some names and addresses. It was a slow process of knocking on doors and getting people involved. The Black/minority ethnic communities in Wester Hailes are very diverse and we wanted to make sure our outreach work was representative of the communities in the area. We usually went in pairs and our team consisted of bilingual workers. We also provided first-language interpreters when required.*

Q: *Can you give me an example of how the Project enabled local people to shape and determine some of its work?*

Andy: I suppose one example I could share is how we worked together *with local people and agencies around the Adegboye Family Campaign.The situation of the Adegboyes became known to us because of the needs survey. Akin and Teju Adegboye were refugees living in Wester Hailes. Akin was then detained in Saughton Prison. Because the survey included specific questions relating to the area of immigration and asylum, respondents were able to clearly identify any problems or queries they might have had in this area. That was how we met the Adegboye family.*

Q: *What happened next?*

Andy: *I went back to meet Teju Adegboye to discuss the situation. I then met Akin in Saughton Prison. He was being held in detention under the powers of the Immigration Act 1971. We discussed ways in which the Project could support the family. After a period of a month, the family gained enough confidence in the Project to agree to a public campaign.*

Q: *How was this confidence gained?*

Andy: *I think because our case work operates on very clear ground rules. Any action that we take will be first agreed with the family. The family have control over any action that we might take on their behalf.*

The campaign had two specific aims which were the family's priorities. Firstly, to secure Akin's release from detention and secondly to secure asylum for the family in this country. It was agreed by all that the best way to achieve this was through a public campaign to build up both local and wider support.

We explored the extent of support amongst local people. Given that this was the first campaign of this kind in Wester Hailes, there was a question mark as to how strongly the wider community would feel about this issue. The actual scale of support was escellent – more than we realistically expected.

Akin Adegboye was released from detention just before Christmas 1995 and the family secured refugee status at the end of January 1996. They were the first Nigerians to win asylum in Britain since the execution of the playwright Ken Saro-Wiwa. Communities had rallied together, agencies networked and built alliances, Wester Hailes expressed loudly and clearly its abhorrence against racist immigration laws. The campaign was a success.

Q: *The campaign was a success. Why did you feel these were important issues for community workers to engage with?*

Andy: *Issues of inequality and injustice should be central to the concerns of all community workers. Black/minority ethnic communities are largely marginalised . Much community work is currently white-led. Issues of racism are not taken on board as a key component of much community work practice and therefore community workers are not actually addressing one of the central areas of need for the Black/minority ethnic communities.*

Part of the explanation of this is that there are very few Black community workers employed within community work provision. Where they are employed, they tend to be marginalised into short-term funded voluntary sector projects or employed on short-term contracts within local authorities.

Q: *If community work were to assert a radical agenda in the area of challenging racism, what would you say the central features of this might be?*

Andy: *What I think is needed is a shift in power and a commitment to supporting community projects that are genuinely owned and controlled by Black/minority ethnic people. A radical agenda has also to recognise the increasing fragmentation of society and social groups. A radical model based on class alone is no longer adequate, a radical community work agenda is one that is inclusive of issues of gender, disability, sexuality, race and so forth.*

Workers would also need to acknowledge there are professional limits. For example, as a white worker, there may be certain facets of the project work in which it would not be appropriate for me as a white male worker to be engaging directly. In recognising that, the next step would be active recruitment of staff who would be appropriate.

Q: *As a white male community worker, what did you gain from this experience?*

Andy: *I went through so many emotions in supporting the family – from anger to despair. I felt good that I was able to make a difference by using my skills as a community development worker. It was positive to see such large numbers of people, both Black and white working together. This was uplifting.*

Radical Anti-Racist Community Work – Lessons from WHARP

(a) Recognising racism. The Project had thought through its value base and aims. Whilst recognising the importance of individual needs and rights, it located these issues within an understanding of the processes and effects of structural racism.It recognised that racism and related issues such as immigration and nationality impacted on the life-chances of many black/ethnic minority people within Britain today. In the survey, these issues were included as part of the study. The issues did not become lost or subsumed under more generic categories like education and employment. Radical anti-racist community work practice needs to engage with issues of concern to people suffering racism – racial harassment, racist immigration legislation, marginalisation of community languages to name a few.

(b) Non-neutrality. The Project was not afraid to engage with political issues, despite the potential conflicts that could have arisen from funders and managers. It recognised there was no room for sitting on fences. Neutrality, based on professional detachment, did not form part of radical practice. It worked with the communities to define what could be achieved between the centres and margins of power. The project worked to assist a family and community in conflict with the state. Radical community work has to be prepared to work with and within conflict.

(c) Contact making and analysis of need. A community development role was undertaken. The project did not seek to define the issues on behalf of the communities but sought to be informed. In conducting the door-to-door work, the workers became 'in touch' with the real life experiences of people. Radical anti-racist community work practice must be informed by the lived experiences of those that suffer racism. WHARP did not utilise outmoded methods such as talking to community leaders but through its door-to-door outreach made contact with a range of Black people.

Radical community work programmes need to have relevance for the people it aims to provide a service for. Given that the majority of community workers and providers are white-led, there is particular responsibility that contact with Black people are made and dialogues initiated. Accountability must first and foremost be with the victims of racism and then secondly, the wider community and finally the funders.

(d) Conscientization of experience. WHARP staff learnt about the effects of racism from their fieldwork by listening to people whose lives were grounded in the experience of racism. In engaging with the Adegboye campaign, they held public meetings and worked with many local agencies. Through these processes the Adegboye's experience was used as a stimulus for action and to stimulate community awareness of racial oppression. Radical anti-racist community work would utilise experience to educate and awaken the critical consciousness of the people it is working with in order to produce a process of social change. The process here was to awaken the mass to the experience of the oppressed and to educate for action. (see Friere, 1972)

(e) Building community capacity. The project worked with local people to build a campaign in solidarity with the Adegboye family. The issues facing the Adegboye family became issues shared with the wider community of Wester Hailes. Radical anti-racist community work empowers both black and white. It promotes opportunities for collaborative work between people and agencies and creates a politics of solidarity.

(f) Networking. The project drew its learning and support from other community projects already engaging in anti-deportation work both within Scotland and England. Radical anti-racist community work draws its strength from sharing between agencies and communities already engaged in anti-racist work.

(g) Recognising limitations. The staff recognised that work on the ground had to be accessible and appropriate for the communities. This meant having a diverse staff team to work in the field. The importance of having bilingual staff, both male and female was seen as crucial to the work. White workers recognised their professional limitations. Radical anti-racist community work would consider critically how white and black workers should engage with each other professionally. Such a model would also seek to create opportunities for dialogue to take place with the intention of working to create a framework of institutionalised equality.

(h) Recognising diversity. The work done by WHARP aimed to be representative of the different black people within the area. The main issue to be challenged was racism/racial discrimination but the specificities of experiences of different black peoples, whether that be through ethnicity, nationality, culture, religion or language, were considered with equal weighting. The Project did not just work with the majority of minority groupings nor with the most vocal black people.

(i) Obtaining outcomes. Radical anti-racist community work requires to move beyond verbal cleverness, statements of intent and equal opportunities policies. It requires action and outcomes. WHARP worked with the sort of outcomes the people on the receiving end of racism were asking for. In this instance, all its outcomes were achieved. The WHARP outcomes in themselves would not necessarily be construed as radical but the outcomes desired were agreed with direct participation and consultation of those suffering racism. Outcomes do not have to be ambitious, but they need to exist if the hopes of people are not to fade.

Conclusion – what characterises a radical anti-racist community work model of practice?

I would argue that it is a way of thinking and practice which is politicised, which engages in critical appraisal of the status quo and acts for change; not reformist change (an adaptation or remoulding of the old paradigms), but change which improves the life chances of those who have been powerless or marginalised. It operates from a basis that acknowledges structural inequalities, and that racism is not an aberration of history but a construct designed to maintain an unequal structure. Radical anti-racist community work draws its influences from the lived experiences of people who suffer racism and racial oppression.

It would subject experience to reflection and analysis, thereby giving meaning to that experience. For Friere (1972), this involves a process of becoming critically aware of one's reality in a manner which leads to effective action upon it. This is a fundamental role for community workers.

Radical anti-racist community work enables black peoples to empower themselves in ways which would address change in the structures which have continued to subjugate them. Dominant themes in its practice include the redistribution of power from predominantly white-led institutions to a more multicultural, lingual and racial structure. Solidarity work – building alliances between Black and white (recognising that racism is detrimental to all) – is key; engaging in political education and assisting in the channelling of energies and experiences into action. Most importantly, it is premised by a structural analysis of racism and an analysis of power.

Shaw and Crowther (1995) state that making power visible requires critical reflection on both the professional and political agendas shaping practice. An analysis of power and how the power holders utilise these to define community work agendas and social problems must be a prerequisite to radical anti-racist community work. The radical worker can then work with communities to demystify social problems broadening the discourse from one of ethnicity or cultural differences to a discourse of racism in all its guises – personal, cultural and structural.

Radical anti-racist community work is not hierarchal in approach but is grounded in real lives and experiences. Whilst grappling with the theories of 'race' and constructs like racism, it seeks to test these continuously against grassroot experience thereby holding on to some form of relevance for the disempowered and oppressed. It builds networks and encourages active learning which empowers disadvantaged communities and builds on the strengths of communality. It will have the courage to challenge prejudices and injustices of both Black and white communities.

Radical anti-racist community work practice cannot be removed from an analysis of the contemporary cultural and political environment of a New Right agenda. (For an educational analysis of the New Right, see Quicke, 1988). The New Right have declared anti-racism as being too political. Community work, if it is to address British racism and the situation and needs of Black communities, must anticipate and address the difficulties that will arise. We live in a period which has promoted possessive individualism and one in which we have an increasingly coercive state apparatus. We have seen a remarkable toleration of the divergence between the haves and have nots in Scottish life. Consequently, we now live in a society where 'finding' and then 'blaming a victim' has become a political art (see Findlay in this volume). If our community work practice is not to become yet another tool for repression, then we must work critically with communities to reject any form of personal pathology and to create space for communities to explore action against exploitative systems.

Acknowledgements

Special thanks to **Amanda Repo Taiwo Thomson**, Development Officer, University Ethos and Ethnic Minorities Project, **Andy Egan,** Coordinator, Wester Hailes Campaign Against Racism and **Malcolm Parnell,** Community Worker, Moredun, Edinburgh for their valued contributions, thoughts and advice

References

Alibhai, Y. (1994). The great backlash. *In:* S. Dunant, ed. *The War of the Words*. London: Virago, 1994

Arshad, R. and McCrum, M. (1989). Black woman, white Scotland. *In:* A. Brown and D. McCrone, eds. *Scottish Government Yearbook*. Edinburgh University, pp 207-224

Brown,C. and Lawton, J. (1991). *Training for Equality: A Study of Race Relations and Equal Opportunities Training*, London: Policy Studies Institute

Editorial (1995). *Campaign Against Racism and Fascism*. No. 24 (Feb-March), p 3

Dominelli, L. (1994). Women, community work and the state. *In:* Jacob and Popple, eds. *Community Work in the 1990s*. Spokesman

Dunlop, A. (1993). Anti-racist politics in Scotland. *Scottish Affairs*. No. 3, Spring, pp 89-100

Freire, P. (1972). *Pedagogy of the Oppressed*. London. Penguin Books

Hatcher, R. (1987). 'Race' and education: two perspectives for change. *In:* B. Troyna, ed. *Racial Inequality in Education*, London. Tavistock Publications, pp 184 – 200

Haynes, A. (1983). *The State of Black Britain*, London: Root Publishing Ltd

Klein, G. (1993). *Education Towards Race Equality*. London. Cassell, pp 86-9

Malik, K. (1996). Universalism and difference: race and postmodernists. *In: Paradigms of Racism, Race and Class*. 37(3), pp 1-18. London: Institute of Race Relations

Mama. A. (1995). *Beyond the Masks-Race, Gender and Subjectivity*. London. Routledge

Martin, I. (1987). Community education: towards a theoretical analysis. *In:* G.Allen et al, eds. *Community Education: An Agenda for Educational Reform.* Milton Keynes: Open University Press, p 23

Miles, R. and Dunlop, A. (1986). The racialization of politics in Britain: why Scotland is different. *Patterns of Prejudice.* 20(1), pp 23 -33

Mullard, C. (1982) Multicultural education in Britain: from assimilation to cultural pluralism. *In:* J. Tierney, ed. *Race, Migration and Schooling.* London: Holt Education

Ohri, A. and Manning, B. (1982). Racism – the response of community work. *In:* Ohri et al, ed. *Community Work and Racism.* London: Routledge & Kegan Paul, pp 3- 13

Quick, J. (1988). The 'New Right' and education. *The British Journal of Educational Studies.* 26(1), February

Rehman, S. (1994). Race and education – the new challenge. *In:* Lothian Racial Equality Council, *Annual Report.* Edinburgh:LREC, p 43

Rudduck, J. (1986). A strategy for handling controversial issues in secondary schools. *In:* J.Wellington, ed. *Controversial Issues in the Curriculum.* Oxford: Blackwell

Sandel, M. (1994). As quoted in M.Phillips, 'Illiberal Liberalism'. In: S. Dunant, (ed) *The War of the Words.* London: Virago

Sarup, M. (1991). *Education and the Ideologies of Racism.* Stoke-on-Trent: Trentham

Scarman (1982). *The Brixton Disorders,* London: Penguin

Sivanandan, A. (1983). *A Different Hunger: Writings on Black Resistance.* London: Pluto Press

Sivanandan, A. (1985). RAT and the degradation of black struggle. *Race and Class.* 26(4), pp 1-34

Sivanandan, A. (1995). Building unity. *Campaign Against Racism and Fascism*. No. 24 (Feb-March)

Shaw, M. and Crowther, J. (1995). Beyond subversion. *In:* M. Mayo and J. Thompson, ed. *Adult Learning Critical Intelligence and Social Change*. Leicester: NIACE

Troyna, B., ed. (1987). *Racial Inequality in Education*, London: Tavistock Publications

Wainwright, H. (1991). Independent left versus radical right. *Catalyst*. No: 6, Feb-April

Chapter 11: Community Arts: Reconnecting with the Radical Tradition

Barbara Orton

Synopsis

In this essentially historical account of the influences and development of community arts, the author seeks to clarify the purposes behind the use of community arts terminology, as a necessary step towards resisting the commodification and appropriation of culture. In explaining the radical tradition within community arts, she identifies the relationship between social purpose and the production of art, arguing that community arts needs to be re-located within a collective enterprise which develops community and cultural confidence and skills. By using community arts to liberate subjugated voices, she argues, a connection is made with the radical enterprise which was at the heart of the debate which established it as a distinctive activity. In making this reconnection, the chapter explores the contribution which community arts has and can still make to creating the conditions through which the disenfranchised can be heard, drawing from both an international context and experiences and examples from closer to home.

Introduction

Historically, community arts has been seen as marginal to the real issues within communities – health, housing and unemployment – but, since 1980, the policy makers and power brokers seem, on the face of it, to have accorded community arts an increased status. This chapter challenges this perception and sets out to show that, despite an increase in the use of the language of community arts within policy documents, this reflects a misappropriation of the terminology for other purposes rather than an acceptance of democratic participation within the arts. The chapter discusses community arts within the context of historical definitions of art and traces the influences and development of the community arts movement in Scotland since the

1970s. In order to unravel some of the confusion surrounding community arts, I will emphasise purpose as a means of making sense of this increasingly contested use of the term 'community arts' and its terminology. Within the development of community arts it is possible to see the emergence of a radical strand and I explore whether community arts can make a contribution to the challenging of inequality in the 1990s by reconnecting with its more radical roots. In doing so we have to acknowledge the increasingly difficult context which has seen art, along with other industries and activities, being subjected to marketisation and commodification, illustrated by the growing heritage industry finding a niche market for local culture and community arts.

The 'treatment' of the arts: new agendas for old

Williams (1958) notes that definitions of 'art' have evolved significantly throughout time. He draws attention to a medieval view of art as any form of human skill or craft within which you could talk about the art of painting and decorating, for example, and cites Michelangelo as a master of it. This definition of art, linked with artisans and manufacture, survived until the 19th Century when other ideas began to take hold. The Victorians developed romantic notions of art as some kind of superior reality quite separate from manufacture and commentators such as Matthew Arnold, for example, referred to these bourgeoise notions of art as 'sweetness and light', something that had inherent value for education and improvement, not only for themselves but also, benignly, for their workers.

It was this notion of art as an activity for moral improvement, an activity which could enrich, uplift and educate, which was taken up by the Arts Council on its establishment after the Second World War. Local government, as well as central government, took on this historical duty, as Franco Bianchinni (1992) notes, to promote this kind of high art for its uplifting benefits with a view to democratic access; not so much towards participation *in* it, but about education towards an appreciation *of* it. Although this kind of 'traditional' art may be found in communities, it is inevitably placed there by institutions or public bodies, and, even when it is produced there by a local artist, it is seldom the kind of community art referred to below.

The appearance of community arts in the early 1970s was quite different, and signalled an oppositional movement to what were seen as sterile and elitist views of traditional art. Community arts, in this account, contrasted with high art in that it placed emphasis on participation and process, and reflected a view of arts as part of a wider development of cultural renewal and communication between people, where the end product was valued either less, or merely as much as, the process itself. Williams (1958), in his seminal definition, expresses art as a participatory process where 'our descriptions of our experience come to compose of a network of relationships, and all our communication systems, including the arts, are literally parts of our social organisation.... the process of communication is in fact the process of community: the sharing of common meanings and thence common activities and purposes: the offering, reception and comparison of new meanings, leading to the tensions and achievements of growth and change'. He links art to 'community' by identifying them both as part and parcel of a whole communication process between people that constantly shapes and defines the world of the participants in the various exchanges. In this sense community arts is not only a participatory process but one which reflects and contributes to the way of life, and the history and culture of communities.

Although the development of community arts is explored in more detail in the next section, it is important to note here how it has impacted on mainstream policy. Over a period of time the language of community arts has been incorporated into arts policy statements and documents. The Scottish Arts Council, for example, in its Charter for the Arts (1992) whilst still holding on to the notion of 'excellence', acknowledges that 'the traditional, received distinctions between high and popular, professional and amateur, commercial and subsidised are no longer tenable because excellence can be found in all of them, and the social divisiveness associated with such distinctions is no longer acceptable or even relevant'. In wider policy terms, the Scottish Office (1992) acknowledged community arts when it adapted Urban Aid guidelines to include 'support for cultural development' in inner city or community regeneration plans. The Glasgow Development Agency (1992) states 'the arts has played an important role in the creation of confidence, identity and opportunity in many of Glasgow's disadvantaged communities'.

The question which inevitably arises from this acknowledgement of community arts within policy statements is to what extent it reflects a victory – an acceptance of community arts by the establishment – or whether it can simply be explained in terms of a misappropriation of the terminology of community arts for other purposes.

In attempting to answer this question, some light is thrown on the matter by exploring the funding of community arts. Even if key agencies, such as the Scottish Arts Council, now acknowledge community arts at a Policy level, they are still very reluctant to fund it. Arts Council funding which does reach the communities of Scotland usually takes the form of individual artist residencies and commissions for individual artists reflecting their view that the responsibility for much of the funding of community arts lies at the doors of local authorities. These local authorities however, who despite having also picked up the language of community art, are still as Bianchinni (1992) has shown, heavily influenced by traditional definitions of art, or a view that seeks to shift community arts to meet economic rather than cultural objectives (as within regeneration policies).

Any gains, or appearance of gains, made by the community arts movement and the wider arts debate between process and product must, however, be seen in the context of the wider changes which have taken place within society and which have, in different ways, affected both the ideas and practices of traditional high art as well as the less well esteemed community arts. Both have been affected by the restructuring of capitalism which has taken place since the late 1970s and the creation of new internal and external markets (see Player, Cooke, Shaw in this volume). As large areas of activity such as health and education have been subjected to the market process, it is hardly surprising that the arts, including community arts, have not been cocooned from these developments. A major impact on community arts has been the marketisation of culture with local or community culture being packaged into potential cultural industries.

Local authorities, many still clinging to notions of taking 'high art' into the communities, have jumped aboard rather than resisted these marketisation processes. Simon Frith (1992) shows how local authorities, in addition to confusing community arts or community culture with popular or mass market culture, have tried 'to define local heritage itself as the object of consumption, as a communal heritage, competing with other heritages in the leisure market, as each city rewrites its history in terms of a trademark, a sales point, a market niche....' He goes on to point out that even within Labour controlled councils, 'what started as a progressive move, a challenge to "elite culture", a determination to take popular values and culture seriously, ends in reaction, in a sentimental story of a "people" who never existed'.

It has been argued, by those involved in community arts, that the ambiguities around the term 'community arts' and the language associated with it has assisted the commodification processes outlined above and allowed political initiatives to append community arts to economic and ideological objectives. If community arts are to be reconnected with the radical traditions from which it developed then we need not only to define and re-apply it, but to critically review it in the light of the current context, drawing out its failures as well as its successes.

Community arts and radical purposes: reflections on practice

The 1970s saw the emergence of the most recent of the community arts movements, in keeping with the new mood of libertarianism, classlessness and creativity prevalent at the time. The main impetus for this development came from those young artists, generally just out of art school, who were disaffected by the art of the gallery and concert hall, who were determined to break out of what they saw as the constraints of established arts practice and relate to a wider world. Influenced by the radical nature of both student politics and wider society, some consciously sought links with various social and political organisations including the Labour and Trade Union movement, CND, tenants' groups and other campaigning organisations of that period.

A number of artists, for example, chose to work as individual artists with the Labour movement and left wing political parties, using new media technology to break away from traditional arts, eg. Peter Kennard and his anti-war photo-montages, the banners of Ken Sprague and the fine work of John Gorman in his book 'Banner Bright' (1986) focusing on the art of Trade Union banners. But, for the artists who wanted to re-locate art and produce it collectively with 'the people', it meant going to where they were – the housing schemes, the local halls and centres, the playgrounds, the parks and public spaces – in an effort to break away from the individualistic establishment world of what they saw as dominant 'bourgeoise' arts and culture. In a bid to identify with the people and the places, they called themselves 'community artists'. Their purpose was not to present art to be appreciated or passively consumed but, rather, to look on art as a creative process that everyone could and had a right to take part in. As community artists they were interested in re-claiming the public spaces for the creation of a popular art, defined as art of the people. This radical stance or operational framework was essentially libertarian, oppositional; more about being liberated *from* institutions than working *inside* them. Taking an anti-materialist stance, they were also reacting against prevalent views which regarded art as a commodity whose sole value was the price for which it could be bought and sold, and they strove to move away from this market relationship.

A combination of radical libertarianism, social concern and innovative arts practices, then, all contributed to the development of 'Community Arts': an arts practice that demanded a direct and collective relationship between artists and people; egalitarian in giving the opportunity for everyone to have a cultural voice and to be able to represent themselves; relevant art in a social sense; participatory rather than consumable; challenging and raising questions about the role of art in particular and the dominant ideas of society in general.

Community arts and policy: an ambivalent context

This movement could not have flourished, however, unless there had been some institutional developments which supported and reaffirmed this practice. An Association of Community Artists was set up in 1972 who began to lobby for official state recognition in order to secure funding for this new work. In response, an Arts Council working party on community arts was established in June 1974, which recommended that the Arts Council of Great Britain set up a Community Arts Panel (1975) to fund various community arts groups and projects that had emerged as a result of local initiatives. The movement was officially recognised by the mid 1970s in England, and both the Scottish and Welsh Arts Councils were encouraged to consider appropriate means of supporting community arts. The response of the Scottish Arts Council was to set up the Mixed Programmes Committee to deal with grant aid and support to the sector.

These developments were not, however, uniformly welcomed, and many of the community artists regarded them as the first steps in the institutionalisation and 'professionalisation' of community arts. They feared that their work would be led by funding priorities or that they would be drawn into state policies which were more about 'managing' problems than solving them.

When these socially-concerned artists, with their own theories and practices, 'hit' the communities of Scotland , they encountered not only other 'professional workers', many of whom were involved in the emerging practices of community development, but community organisations and activists who had begun developing their own ideas on 'the arts' and how to use them. A famous example of the latter was the Craigmillar Festival Society (CFS), an organisation from one of Edinburgh's 'peripheral' housing estates. Community arts, as Crummy (1992) argues, was not simply about the community asserting its democratic right of access to existing traditional art (eg. championing the right of local children to have violin lessons or challenging the inaccessability of much of Edinburgh's establishment art) but about the opportunity for the community to participate in the creative processes of producing their own art. Crucially, for the Craigmillar Festival Society, community arts was not seen as an end in itself but as a way of raising individual community and cultural confidence which complemented their other activities such as campaigning on housing, social welfare, education and economic development issues. The CFS argued that, in this form, community arts was instrumental in building up skills and powers of expression within individuals, enabling local people to feel and develop a sense of worth, identity, pride and confidence which transferred into other areas of individual's lives (whether it be standing up to doctors or negotiating rent rebates). At a broader level it also crucially, provided the foundation for collective action around issues of concern within the community.

The demands made on the artists by assertive communities, (distinct to the Scottish experience) together with the diverse influences of other professional workers, created tensions which some of the community artists found both artistically limiting and difficult to deal with. Moreover, the existence, within communities, of agendas which were wider than simply countering dominant attitudes towards art, led some community artists into territory within which they were distinctly uneasy. A particular case in point was the experience of artists 'in residence' placed in communities by the Scottish Arts Council and other funding bodies who believed that their talents and skills would somehow 'rub off' on people and enlighten communities. Braden (1978) vividly describes the misery some of these artists experienced, being totally unequipped with the language, or ironically, communication skills to reach the people with whom they were supposed to be working. This was a far cry from the garret, and arts workers in this context often found themselves instead involved in issues of local control, the management of resources and democracy as they tried to apply their aesthetic to working class communities throughout the country.

Influences and alliances

In this sense community arts developed, not along any single path but from a fusion of varying influences and practices. Confusion existed over the language and the meaning of 'art', whilst the purposes of community arts and artists' intervention in communities were increasingly contested. The values and agendas of funding agencies, projects and individual workers also added to the debate as did the impact of community perspectives and other professional practices. All these factors contributed to what could be described as a 'battleground of practice' throughout the 1970s and into the 1980s, but from which a radical community arts practice began to emerge.

It was perhaps the fusion of this emerging community arts movement with the growing interest in community development, prevalent within many communities in the 1970s which offered the most radical opportunities. Community development, which placed emphasis on participatory neighbourhood work, developing skills, knowledge and experience to enable local people to collectively better conditions for themselves was influencing the thinking and practice of a range of professional workers and it was, perhaps, inevitable that they would impact on some of those involved in community arts. Inspired by the Craigmillar Festival Society and other such community organisations, community arts were seen to offer possibilities and opportunities towards the development of organised communities capable of taking action around issues such as housing, health and poverty. Community arts, in this sense, was regarded as a useful tool in the building up of individual and collective confidence and skills that allowed people to communicate effectively, and express themselves and their realities in potentially very powerful ways. These activities drew creatively on drama, street theatre, visual art, music and photography, and the creative potential within community arts attracted professional workers who were not necessarily trained 'artists' who, in turn, added other skills and practices to this evolving area of activity.

The arts workers, more familiar with the concept or practice of developmental work, probably fared better than the artists with their own particular agendas, being able to draw on their experience and training and placing emphasis on working towards 'organisation' as much as working with art. For some workers the aims of community arts were extended beyond the production of art with groups to creating the conditions for communities to produce it themselves, for their own purposes. This included assisting communities to set up arts groups and organisations, and encouraging the development of arts or 'communications' resources within neighbourhoods such as video projects, print workshops, and so on. Communities were encouraged to link arts into campaigns, around local issues of concern which, in turn, became a focus for galas, festivals and other cultural activities. In this sense, community arts was seen, not as a radical activity in itself, but possessing the potential for radicalism when linked in a relevant and appropriate way to other community activites, contributing fun and creativity to political campaigns and direct action.

A relatively small number of community arts workers, influenced by the radical analysis of the Community Development Projects (see Cooke in this volume) with its emphasis on linking and alliance building between community groups and with the Labour movement, questioned the limitations of the localised nature of much community art. They therefore attempted to explore possible ways in which community arts could contribute to those linking processes, seeking to develop community arts within the general development of a radical community work practice. For example, the community-based Pilton Video Project, from a housing estate in North Edinburgh, produced a number of short videos for campaigning trade unionists and the anti-apartheid movement. In the same estate community artists developed working relationships with Edinburgh Trades Council.

Similarly, a visual artist working in the Easterhouse area of Glasgow developed a local visual arts resource which had both community accountablity and strong links with the Labour movement throughout the 1980s. The Cranhill Arts Projects, as it was called, provided a service to the local community by producing a local newsheet and offering training courses; opportunities which were often generated by local community and labour movement contacts. Interestingly, the Project consciously fought shy of the community arts label preferring to identify themselves with working class culture and visual arts. They succeeded in producing high profile art ranging from community photography exhibitions and postcards which depicted life in Cranhill and beyond, to large dynamic posters and contemporary silk screen banners for trade unions and political campaigns.

It is interesting to note that, whilst the Cranhill Project was highly successful, its development as an arts resource for the area was limited by a lack of funding, as it found itself caught in a no win situation: the arts institutions ultimately refused to take them seriously because they were community based, whereas the local authorities viewed them as having developed beyond their community remit. Whilst the Labour movement understood their wider collective remit, the Project's progress in this sphere of activity was inextricably linked with the declining fortunes of the Labour movement throughout the 1980s. Whilst some attempts by community arts workers at linking resulted in productive relationships with the Labour movement throughout this period, others could at best be described as uneasy – the spontaneous nature of community art not sitting well with the hierarchical bureaucracies of the Trade Unions. These difficult experiences contrasted markedly with the more productive attempts to link with the less formalised structures and more open organisational forms of the newer social movements.

Liberating voices

The Cranhill Arts Project exemplifies those forms of community art which take account of Gramsci's idea of 'cultural hegemony'. In arguing for a more just and democratic society, Gramsci (1971) stresses the value of the lived experience of all in countering the cultural domination of the many by the few. This domination, Gramsci argues, is reinforced by the ruling classes' own propaganda and assisted by the Marxist notion of 'false consciousness' which portrays these beliefs as normal, 'common sense', natural or right. Even the hearts and minds of potential 'dissidents' can be caught, conditioned to accept, or censor themselves to accept, a consciousness or explanation which may be against their own interests. In this sense community arts has the potential not only to offer arts, media and communication skills to highlight the issues and problems faced by the community, but for working class people in general to create representations of their own realities, expressed in image, form and language. This process then contributes to a greater awareness, and more value being attached to their own cultural heritage which, in turn, begins to challenge or undermine the state's cultural hegemony. Within this territory, the Cranhill Project can be seen as recognising the need not only to encourage participation within the arts and the use of the arts as a medium to highlight issues and problems which they faced but, importantly, to link community with class. In the same way that the Cranhill Arts Project allied themselves to the Labour and Trade Union movement of the 1980s, we can see similarly how community arts has, and can, work in a similar way with the newer social movements of the last twenty years. The women's, gay and lesbian, disabled, anti-racist and environmental movements have, each in their own way, challenged aspects of the cultural hegemony and made creative use of the arts and media in promoting their respective causes.

The importance of this notion of creating the conditions for the voices of the dispossessed to be heard, and its important role within political movements, has also been acknowledged internationally. Havel, for example has referred to these processes in Czechoslavakia as the 'power of the powerless'. He explains how the people of Czechoslavakia refused to accept the order of the state and used the arts to re-define and re-name the world as they saw it. This was, he claims, the very foundation of the 'Velvet Revolution'.

Within community arts we need constantly to consider the medium, as well as the message. In addition to retaining those elements of innovation and creativity which have characterised community arts in the past we need to add the qualities of boldness and confidence, taking our participatory processes and sense of purpose into, what is, the most powerful medium available today. In applying the Gramscian argument for creating the conditions through which the disenfranchised will be heard today, we need to recognise and challenge the almost total lack of access to the media as being a prime factor in the silencing of alternative 'cultural voices'. Advances in technology have paved the way for communities to challenge the commercialism and centralised control of mainstream television by reasserting TV as a potential 'public space' where groups and people within and between cultures can talk to each other, discussing the issues of the day and creating symbols, images, languages and meanings for themselves.

In Brazil, for example local media workers use public squares to screen highly engaging video on the issues of the day from 'outside broadcast' vans and, whilst alternative television, video and film projects are not a new idea, they have, in recent years become more urgent, necessary and linked to liberation movements to counter the growing commercialism and corporate control of the media. In Peru and Argentina, there are whole networks of 'community' TV stations, broadcasting with low power transmitters to their own localities and in Chile, a highly developed and effective video distribution network has found a sizeable audience for the last 15 years.

Inspirational examples of this work closer to home are groups like 'Small World', an alternative news agency in London, which uses broadcast quality Hi-8 video and camcorders to film on-the-spot coverage of local resistance such as the anti-motorway campaigns. They both sell their dramatic footage to the news networks and use it themselves on their own alternative news networks (national and international video cassette distribution networks).

Back in the street, carnival can also be looked at from this perspective. Whilst on the one hand it is a time of celebration and enjoyment, carnival can also be regarded as a communal festival with deep and profound meanings as embodied, for example in the Masque. In their individual costumes and group scenarios masque dancers are expressing and making statements about themselves, each other and the times in which we live. There are also fascinating parallels to be made with Shetland's own 'Up Helly Aa!'

Conclusion

The previous sections have described how community arts began as a reaction by artists to the elitism of traditionally perceived art production and in opposition to art as a product. These artists brought to communities ideas, skills and, above all, a commitment to processes of wider participation in the production of the arts even if that was at the expense of the product. It was, however, when these developments fused with community development processes within some of the more organised communities that radical opportunities became apparent within community arts: art which had a social and political purpose. It was therefore, the purposes to which community arts was put which determined its nature – community arts is as well able to be used as a tool for social control as it is for radical social purposes.

It has been shown that in the 1980s a number of community arts workers recognised the importance of links being developed between communities and wider progressive political movements (such as the Labour and Trade Union movement) and attempted to reflect this in their practice, reflecting wider community work aims of the time. But, arguably, the most consistent and telling contribution which community arts has, and can, make in a radical sense is when it identifies with issues of voice and representation, in the Gramscian sense, assisting local people to name and represent the validity of their own culture and the authentic expression of their own values. In doing so, opportunities arise for local people, groups, and communities to connect with those aspects of the Labour movement and those aspects of the new social movements which are also counter-hegemonic in nature.

In Scotland we can take inspiration from working class artists such as the writers James Kelman and Tom Leonard who have defiantly taken a stand against dominant narratives, and persisted in writing in a 'local' voice, using the living language which reflects their own working class reality but with a universalism that resists the charge of parochalism. They have had to deal with a lack of status for their language in much the same way that black writers have struggled for status in their colonised countries, and whose refusal to write in the language of their 'oppressors' has often played a vital role in liberation movements.

While it could be said that community arts has created a higher profile for itself in the last few years and can now move between localities and mainstream, depending on form and content, it is important that these 'successes' in an artistic sense, should not obscure the broader social purpose of community arts if it is to retain a radical edge. If we are considering community arts in terms of political change, then, it has to be regarded as more than offering opportunities for people to 'flower'. The 'new territory' for radical practice within community arts should continue to involve working to shift the balance by resisting the agendas set by dominant interests within society, albeit in a changing context. The 'commodification' of local history and local culture in the 1990s presents both challenges and opportunities for community arts to reclaim and reassert 'alternative' histories and cultures which reflect the experience of the majority of disenfranchised people. This can only be done by community arts workers engaging with these histories and cultures; by listening and developing ideas rather than imposing them and by consciously seeking out opportunities to link those community histories and cultures with each other, with social movements and other forces of progressive social change. In this sense community arts can begin to challenge the power relation of the market, rather than simply reproduce it.

Whether community arts is practised in local communities or within the medium of television, it has the potential to provide real opportunities for local voices to be heard on issues and concerns which affect them, as well as providing a means to forge links between real lived experience and wider issues. It is a project which should be at the centre of 'cultural politics' in Scotland, releasing and invigorating the voices of oppressed groups and, in doing so, contributing towards an energised democratic society.

(This chapter is an edited version of a longer (as yet unpublished) article which covers the theory and practice of community arts and the author's experiences as a community arts worker in more detail).

References

Bianchinni, F. (1992) *Paper 40 – Discussion paper on 'Urban Cultural Policy' for the Arts and Media National Strategy*. Arts Council of Great Britain

Braden, S. (1978). *Artists and People*. Routledge and Kegan Paul

Crummy, H. (1992). *Let the People Sing*. H. Crummy

Frith, S. (1992). *Paper 28 – Discussion paper on 'Popular Culture' for the Charter for the Arts in Scotland*. Scottish Arts Council.

Glasgow Development Agency (1992). Quoted by P. Vestri in Arts Council Publication, *Changing Places – The Arts in Scotland's Urban Areas*.

Gorman, J. (1986). *Banner Bright*. Scorpion Publishing Ltd.

Gramsci, A. (1971). *Prison Notebooks*. Lawrence and Wishart

Scottish Arts Council (1992). *Charter for the Arts in Scotland*. Scottish Arts Council

Scottish Office (1992). *Guidelines for the Urban Programme*. Scottish Office.

Williams, R. (1958) *Culture and Society: 1780-1958*. Penguin

Contributors

Rowena Arshad has extensive community work experience, was co-ordinator of Lothian's Multicultural Education Centre, and is currently a lecturer in Equity and Rights at Moray House Institute, Edinburgh.

Chik Collins is a lecturer in Politics at the University of Paisley. Prior to this he worked in both the public and voluntary housing sectors. He has worked with a number of tenants' and community groups addressing housing and urban policy issues. More recently, he has collaborated with Jim Lister in contributing to debates about the future of community work.

Ian Cooke has been a community worker with both Strathclyde Region's Social Work Department and Lothian Region's Community Education Department. As Senior Community Education Worker in Craigroyston Community High School, he explored the community school as a base for community development, and is currently Project Manager with the Pilton Partnership, a community work project located in the north of Edinburgh. He is a member of the editorial group of Concept Journal, the Scottish journal of contemporary debate in the field of community education.

Mick Doyle, Jenny Smith, Isobel Wilson, Douglas Erdman, Sharon Donohoe and **Ann Cummings.** The contributors have had a range of community work experience spanning some 16 years, within both the voluntary and local authority setting. They have been involved in developing campaigning work with private, local authority and Scottish Homes tenants' groups. All are members of **The National Workers' Housing Forum** which was established in 1987 as an informal network for housing and community workers assisting tenants' groups throughout Scotland. The Workers' Forum offers support, information and training on issues relating to the Housing (Scotland) Act 1988, and subsequent developments including Stock Transfer. It also has links to the National Tenants' Movement and offers what support it can to this organisation. Membership is on the basis of how much time any worker can give to the network.

John Findlay has over 20 years community work experience, first with Strathclyde Regional Council Social work department and, currently, as Director of 'One Plus: One Parent Families', Glasgow.

Jim Lister has worked for the past twenty years in a variety of community development settings including a worker co-operative in the north of England, Hamilton (Lanarkshire) and the Palestinian community of Il Ajami. During the past 13 years he has worked in the former G.E.A.R. Area (east end of Glasgow) and, most recently, in the Strathclyde Region and Glasgow District Council funded neighbourhood initiative serving Cuthelton, Lilybank and Newbank. He has worked with community organisations, including tenants' associations, on issues relating to the restructuring of the economy, and the built environment (including housing).

Jane Meagher has worked for the Lothian Region Community Education Service since 1980 in a range of settings: in a community centre, a community school and as an area youth work specialist. She is currently the Training Officer for the Community Education Service. She has also been active in the Women's Movement since the late 1970s. She is a member of the editorial group of Concept Journal, the Scottish journal of contemporary debate in the field of community education.

Barbara Orton worked as an arts worker in Pilton, Edinburgh, for a considerable number of years, during which time she helped establish, and was involved in, Pilton Video Project. She was then employed by the Festival Unit in Glasgow District Council, to develop community-based contributions as part of the city's designation as 'European City of Culture' in 1990. She is now an independent producer and director in both broadcast television and in the local and international alternative TV sector, and does freelance teaching in community arts.

Margaret Petrie is Co-Ordinator of Access Ability Lothian and has previously worked as an adult education tutor. She also has substantial experience of work with young people. She is a member of the editorial group of Concept Journal, the Scottish journal of contemporary debate in the field of community education.

John Player is a community education fieldworker in Wester Hailes, Edinburgh, for Lothian Regional Council's Community Education Service. He has previously worked for Edinburgh Voluntary Organisation's Council and Strathclyde Region's Social Work Department. He is a member of the editorial group of Concept Journal, the Scottish journal of contemporary debate in the field of community education.

Mike Rosendale has been involved in community work since the early 1970s, initially as an activist in tenants' associations in Aberdeen, as a community worker in the voluntary sector and in Lothian Regional Council's Community Education Service. He is currently Community Education Manager of the South West Edinburgh area.

Mae Shaw has had a range of community work experience within the voluntary sector, extending over fifteen years. In London, she worked with Camden Task Force, developing campaigning work with pensioners' organisations. As a community worker with Tenants and Workers Information Network in Edinburgh, she worked largely with tenants' organisations on housing issues. She is currently employed as a lecturer in Community Work at Moray House Institute of Education, Edinburgh. She is also Executive Editor of Concept, the Scottish journal of contemporary debate in the field of community education.

Lyn Tett first became involved in community education as an activist campaigning for children's play provision. Since then she has worked in adult education in Argyll and Bute where she had a particular interest in women's issues. and held the post of assistant director responsible for adult education and training at the Scottish Community Education Council. She is currently Director of Community Education at Moray House Institute.